975.8
L

1. Ga- Social life and customs

G

SEQUOYAH REGIONAL LIBRARY SYSTEM

3 8749 0006 6741 8

10649920

Georgia Scenes, &c.

GEORGIA SCENES
CHARACTERS,
INCIDENTS &c.

in the first half century of the Republic

by a native Georgian,
Augustus B. Longstreet

introduction by Richard Harwell

THE BEEHIVE PRESS
Savannah

GILMER CO. LIB.

87072

© 1975 by The Beehive Press

LCC Number 74-22693

Contents

Illustrations

Introduction

GEORGIA SCENES is a landmark of American literary history, a pioneer expression of authentic folk humor and a forthright picture of frontier Georgia. Nearly a century and a half after its first publication it stands as an informative and entertaining record of the life of the common people of the South during the early years of the American Republic.

Augustus Baldwin Longstreet consciously took the risk of writing for posterity. His brief preface to the *Scenes* begins: "The following sketches were written, rather in the hope that chance would bring them to light, when time would give them an interest, than in the belief that they would afford any interest to the readers of the present day. I knew, however, that the chance of their surviving the author would be increased in proportion to their popularity upon their first appearance; and therefore I used some little art in order to recommend them to the readers of my own times."[1] In "The Gander Pulling," describing an incident at Augusta in 1798, he excuses himself for explaining the early geography of the town, saying: "Since it has been predicted by a man for whose opinions I entertain the profoundest respect (especially since the prediction), that my writings will be read with increased interest a hundred years to come . . . I will take the liberty of dropping a word here to the curious reader of the year 1933."[2] Longstreet succeeded in creating a book that not only appealed to his own time but one which has become a historical and literary classic.

*   *   *

Augustus Baldwin Longstreet was born in Augusta, Georgia, September 22, 1790.[3] His earliest schooling was at home, but from 1808 to 1810 he attended the academy of Dr. Moses Waddel in Willington, South Carolina. In 1811, following in the footsteps of his friend John C. Calhoun, he entered Yale College. He completed his studies at Yale in 1813 and, still following Calhoun's example, entered Reeve and Gould's law school in nearby Litchfield.

He returned to his home state late in 1814 and studied the specifics of its law for a while in Augusta. He was there admitted to the Georgia bar on May 26, 1815. He began his practice in the state's middle circuit and soon became the familiar of such stalwarts of Georgia's political and literary history as George B. Gilmer, John M. Berrien, Duncan G. Campbell, John Clarke, Augustin S. Clayton, William H. Crawford, William C. Dawson, John M. Dooley, John Forsyth, Oliver Hillhouse Prince, George M. Troup, and Richard Henry Wilde. Longstreet's travels to the courts of his district regularly took him to Greensboro. There he fell in love with Frances Eliza Parke and married her in March, 1817. Immediately thereafter he moved his residence from Augusta to Greensboro.

In 1821 Longstreet was elected representative in the

Georgia legislature from Greene County. The next year he was made, by vote of the two branches of the legislature, Judge of the Superior Court of the new Ocmulgee District. His career as a judge lasted only three years. In 1825 Longstreet's friend Troup was elected governor, but control of the General Assembly went to supporters of Clarke. Although Longstreet had been elected to the judgeship during Clarke's term as governor, he was, along with virtually all of Troup's supporters, now refused reelection.

Perhaps the Judge's failure to be reelected proceeded from other reasons than mere partisan politics. He had served well as a judge. He had engaged his growing fortune and his wife's in successful farming in Greene County. He was popular among his associates at the bar, was awarded an honorary degree as Master of Arts by the University of Georgia in 1823, and was officially praised by the Grand Jury of Morgan County in 1824. In that year he announced for Congress. There was no doubt that he would be elected. But in September, 1824, events occurred which changed the course of his life.

Within two days of one another Longstreet's mother-in-law and his eldest child were taken by death. Longstreet immediately withdrew from the campaign for Congress and gave way to deep melancholy. Recovery was slow, but, following the example of his wife's stepfather, he sought solace in religion. "I would," he later wrote, "give a thousand worlds, thought I, if I could believe the Scriptures as that man does; their fruits are lovely, to say the least of them. And may it not be that my unbelief is my own fault? I am very ignorant of the Scriptures, I never bestowed an hour's study on them, with the honest aim of ascertaining their truth in all my life. . . . I commenced studying the Scriptures in earnest, praying God if they really were true that I might be convinced of their truth. . . . All my doubts soon vanished, and I became a thorough believer in Christianity."[4]

Longstreet returned to his usual activities, but much of the zest was gone from life in Greensboro. He moved his family to Augusta in 1827 and there continued to practice law and to farm. The farming did not prosper, but his endeavors as a lawyer did. He entered into partnership with William W. Mann, a connection which Charles J. Jenkins joined early in 1832. Mann was a local literary figure of considerable ability, and Jenkins was a rising statesman. In such company it was pleasant and easy for the Judge to maintain his interest in politics and indulge himself in writing, as the inevitable phrase goes, for his own amusement.

It was in Augusta that *Georgia Scenes* was begun; at least it began to be put on paper there. Longstreet had doubtless mulled over the *Scenes* in his rides from court to court, and some of them must have been narrated to companions of long evenings in country inns. The first of the *Scenes* to be published was "The Ball." It appeared in *The Southern Recorder*, Milledgeville, in 1832.[5] Eleven of the sketches were printed in that paper before their author purchased and commenced editing his own newspaper, *The State Rights Sentinel*, in Augusta. Longstreet transferred publication of the *Scenes* to the *Sentinel* in April, 1834. In 1835 he collected the sketches that had been printed to that time and issued them in an unpretentious book with the imprint of his own paper's office.

The Judge continued his interests in his profession as a

lawyer and in politics as a disciple of Calhoun. He continued his literary self-indulgence with the composition and
publication of nearly a dozen more Georgia scenes. But his
religious interests soon got an upper hand. In 1838 he became a Methodist minister and the next year was named
President of fledgling Emory College. He served as President of Emory until 1848, when he resigned to accept a
similar post at Centenary College, recently removed from
Mississippi to Louisiana. After only a few months of less
than complete success there, Longstreet left Centenary to
return to Georgia. He was, however, elected President of
the University of Mississippi (a post which he had been un-
officially and vainly promised the year before) and, after a
summer's visit in Georgia, took up his duties at Oxford,
Mississippi, in September, 1849.

Until controversy marred the end of his tenure, Longstreet engaged in successful college administration in Mississippi. His years there were fruitful also in well-managed
investments in land, and he continued an interest in politics, especially in areas where religion and politics met, for
he considered himself primarily a preacher, a minister on
special assignment as an educator. He opposed the Mississippi Whigs and, particularly, the growth of Know-Noth-
ingism. By 1855 the intensity of this interest cornered him
into a position as awkward as it was rectitudinous. "I saw
this 'political party,' " he wrote, "while protesting aloud
against my teaching of politics in the University, whispering
the students of my charge into its midnight gatherings, and
there binding them by oath upon oath to everlasting fidelity
to its own particular creed. I now spoke out boldly in my
own defence and against the party; not against its princi-

ples, but against its mode of propagating them. They assailed me on all sides and in all modes. Not one of them gravely answered my objections to the Know-Nothing discipline and dealings. They chose rather to assail me personally in language as unbecoming to them as it was undeserved by me. Even my literary *bagatelle*, the amusement of my idle hours five and twenty years ago, was held up to view as a test of my fitness morally and intellectually for the sacred office and responsible station to which I have been called."[6] In the summer of 1856 Longstreet resigned as President of the University at Oxford and retired to Abbeville, Mississippi.

His retirement was short-lived. In November, 1857, he was offered the presidency of the University of South Carolina and undertook its duties in Columbia in January, 1858. He succeeded to a difficult administrative situation which, with the help of his fervor for the South and the approaching Southern Confederacy, he eventually managed to turn. He exhorted his students to support secession. Then, when secession became fact, he frantically pleaded for prudence and patience: "Why . . . in the name of God, bring on a war of such fearful consequences! If you mean to hold Fort Moultrie, I implore you let the first shot come from the enemy."[7] The University held together through the first months of war; but, when its students dispersed to the Confederate Army after the capture of Port Royal in November, 1861, its President had no recourse but to resign and to return once more to Mississippi.

Longstreet spent the war years in Mississippi, where his old home at Oxford was eventually burned by marauding soldiers. He took refuge at Columbus and Oxford, Georgia, and visited also Charleston, South Carolina, and Enon,

Alabama. He was a chaplain of the Georgia Militia but active only with his pen. The uncle of General James Longstreet and the father-in-law of L. Q. C. Lamar, he was privy to the inner circles of the Confederates' power and was an intense partisan of their cause.

Longstreet served a long and useful life. His distinction as a lawyer was local, but his contributions to education were regional. His general eminence as a minister was subordinated to his work as college president, but it was considerable. He was a delegate to the Methodist General Conference of 1844, the fateful meeting at which debate over slavery split the denomination into two branches. In 1860 he was honored with appointment as the only United States delegate to an International Statistical Congress in London—an unfortunate honor, however, for Longstreet withdrew from the Congress on learning of the presence of a Negro delegate from Canada. In private business he was generally successful, though as a planter and farmer he tended to neglect details and did not prosper in agriculture as well as he did in trading land.

The end of the war brought a final and different retirement. The Longstreets had been severely reduced in fortune but had not been impoverished by the war. Life in postwar Mississippi was pleasant, if not of the former standard of luxury. It was full of reminiscence, and the Judge's pen ran freely of the old ink of politics and religion. In 1870 he was once again considering a removal to Georgia, to the presidency of a law school proposed for Macon. This time death made the decision. He died in Oxford, Mississippi, July 9, 1870.

*   *   *

All his life Longstreet wrote, but *Georgia Scenes* is his single significant contribution to literature. He knew the Georgians he described, he grew up among them, and he saw them at the courts throughout middle Georgia. He had a good ear and was known to his friends as one who could tell an anecdote with inimitable style. He wrote of the country matrons who appear in "A Sage Conversation": "I cannot ... ridicule them myself, nor bear to hear them ridiculed in my presence. And yet, I am often amused at their conversations; and have amused *them* with a rehearsal of their own conversations, taken down by me when they little dreamed I was listening to them. Perhaps my reverence for their character, conspiring with a native propensity to extract amusement from all that passes under my observation, has accustomed me to pay a uniformly strict attention to all they say in my presence."[8] In his preface, Longstreet says the *Scenes* "consist of nothing more than fanciful *combinations* of *real* incidents and characters; and throwing into those scenes, which would otherwise be dull and insipid, some personal incident or adventure of my own, real or imaginary, as it would best suit my purpose—usually *real*, but happening at different times and under different circumstances from those in which they are here represented. I have not always, however, taken this liberty. Some of the scenes are as literally true as the frailties of memory would allow them to be."[9]

The sketches of *Georgia Scenes* are by Longstreet's own evidence and by other contemporaneous evidence, though scarce it is, accurate representations of the people of northeastern Georgia—"Upper Georgia" as it was then called—with a single excursion to Savannah on the coast and another west to LaGrange. His characters are frontiersmen of the first generation of the Republic, separated from the Savannahians and other low-country gentry by a hundred miles of little-developed pine barrens and by as much or more of tradition and background. Many of these upper Georgians had come to the southernmost of the British colonies when former Indian lands north of Saint Paul's Parish were opened to settlers after the treaty of Augusta in 1773. Generally not landowners in Virginia and the Carolinas, these pioneers set out to establish themselves in new country. Under Elijah Clarke they defeated the British in the Battle of Kettle Creek and helped establish a nation. If in *Georgia Scenes* they and their progeny appear as plain, hardy countryfolk, it is only fair to say that Longstreet did not think of them as members of some lower class. He saw them as the sturdy stock of the frontier, robust men and women indulging in practical jokes, hearty frivolities, and bone-cracking sports.

When *Georgia Scenes* was published in 1835 it took on a life of its own, far beyond the author's expectations. Its greatest boost came in a long, clumsy, but very favorable review by Edgar Allan Poe in the *Southern Literary Messenger* for March, 1836, concluding: "We will give . . . this very humorous and very clever book . . . a niche in our library as a sure omen of better days for the literature of the South."[10]

The book has reached us anonymously . . . yet it is most heartily welcome. The author, whoever he is, is a clever fellow, imbued with a spirit of truest humor, and endowed, moreover, with an exquisitely discriminative and penetrating understanding of *character* in general, and of Southern character in particular. . . . Seriously—if this book were printed in England it would make the fortune of its author. . . . Seldom—perhaps never in our lives—have we laughed as immoderately over any book as over the one now before us. If these *scenes* have produced such efferts upon *our* cachinnatory nerves—upon *us* who are not "of the merry mood," and, moreover, have not been unused to the perusal of somewhat similar things—we are at no loss to imagine what a hubbub they would occasion in the uninitiated regions of Cockaigne. . . . But that the publication will *succeed*, in the book-selling sense of the word, is problematical. Thanks to the long indulged literary supineness of the South, her presses are not as apt in putting forth a *saleable* book as her sons are in concocting a wise one.[11]

Perhaps it was Poe's review placed between reviews of two publications by Harper and Brothers that first called *Georgia Scenes* to the attention of that publishing house. At any rate Harper and Brothers brought out a second edition of the *Scenes* in 1840, illustrated with twelve copperplate engravings by E. H. Hyde. That edition was completely reset, with changes in capitalization, spelling, and grammar which fitted Longstreet's book into Harper's "house style." This Beehive Press edition is printed exactly from the text of the 1835 edition, the only one since that date to follow Longstreet's text as he himself first saw it in book form. Obvious printer's errors have been silently corrected.

Each new reader of Longstreet's stories has the privilege of judging *Georgia Scenes*, but the last word of introduction should belong to Judge Longstreet himself. "The design of the 'Georgia Scenes,'" its author wrote, "has been wholly misapprehended by the public. It has been invariably received as a mere collection of fancy sketches, with no higher object than the entertainment of the reader, whereas the aim of the author was to supply a chasm in history which has always been overlooked—the manners, customs, amusements, wit, dialect, as they appear in all grades of society to an ear and eye witness of them. . . . I have chosen

the first fifty years of our republic in the course of which
short space of time the society of the Southern States under-
went almost an entire revolution, and at this date hardly a
trace of the society of the first thirty years of the republic is
to be found. To be sure, in writing the 'Georgia Scenes' I
have not confined myself to strictly veracious historic detail; but there is scarcely one word from the beginning to
the end of the book that is not strictly *Georgian.*"[12]

NOTES

1. [Augustus Baldwin Longstreet,] *Georgia Scenes*... (Augusta, Ga.: The S. R. Sentinel Office, 1835), p. iii.

2. Ibid., p. 120. In a footnote Longstreet assigned the prediction to "The Editor of
the 'Hickory Nut.' " The whole is fictitious, *The Hickory Nut* being nonexistent.

3. The biographical information in this introduction is drawn from a number of
standard sources, but principally from John Donald Wade, *Augustus Baldwin Longstreet:
A Study of the Development of Culture in the South* (New York: The Macmillan Company,
1924).

4. Longstreet, "Old Things Become New," in *Nineteenth Century Magazine* (Charleston), 1 (1870), 850.

5. A table of the *Scenes* giving title, paper in which published, and date of publication
appears in Wade, p. 384.

6. Oscar Penn Fitzgerald, *Judge Longstreet: A Life Sketch* (Nashville, Tenn.: Printed
for the Author, 1891), pp. 117–18.

7. [Longstreet,] *Shall South Carolina Begin the War?* (n.p. [1861]), p. 4.

8. Longstreet, *Georgia Scenes*, p. 204.

9. Ibid., p. iii.

10. *Southern Literary Messenger* (Richmond), 11 (1836), 287–92.

11. Ibid., p. 287.

12. Fitzgerald, pp. 164–65.

Preface.

THE following sketches were written, rather in the hope that chance would bring them to light, when time would give them an interest, than in the belief that they would afford any interest to the readers of the present day. I knew, however, that the chance of their surviving the author, would be increased in proportion to their popularity upon their first appearance; and therefore I used some little art in order to recommend them to the readers of my own times. They consist of nothing more than fanciful *combinations* of *real* incidents and characters; and throwing into those scenes, which would be otherwise dull and insipid, some personal incident or adventure of my own, real or imaginary, as it would best suit my purpose—usually *real*, but happening at different times and under different circumstances from those in which they are here represented. I have not always, however, taken this liberty. Some of the scenes are as literally true, as the frailties of memory would allow them to be. I commenced the publication of them, in one of the gazettes of the State, rather more than a year ago; and I was not more pleased than astonished, to find that they were well received by readers generally. For the last six months, I have been importuned by persons from all quarters of the State to give them to the public in the present form. This volume is purely a concession to their in-treaties. From private considerations, I was extremely desirous of concealing the author, and the more effectually to do so, I wrote under two signatures. These have now become too closely interwoven with the sketches, to be separated from them, without an expense of time and trouble which I am unwilling to incur. *Hall* is the writer of those sketches in which *men* appear as the principal actors, and *Baldwin* of those in which *women* are the prominent figures. For the "*Company Drill,*" I am indebted to a friend, of whose labors I would gladly have availed myself oftener. The reader will find in the object of the sketches, an apology for the minuteness of detail into which some of them run; and for the introduction of some things into them, which would have been excluded, were they merely the creations of fancy.

I have not had it in my power to superintend the publication of them, though they issue from a press in the immediate vicinity of my residence. I discovered, that if the work was delayed until I could have an opportunity of examining the proof sheets, it would linger in the press, until the expenses (already large) would become intolerable. Consequently there may be many typographical errors among them, for which I must crave the reader's indulgence.

I cannot conclude these introductory remarks, without reminding those who have taken exceptions to the coarse, inelegant, and sometimes ungrammatical language, which the writer represents himself as occasionally using; *that it is language accommodated to the capacity of the person to whom he represents himself as speaking.*

THE AUTHOR.

GEORGIA THEATRICS.

IF my memory fail me not, the 10th of June, 1809, found me at about 11 o'clock in the forenoon, ascending a long and gentle slope, in what was called "The Dark Corner" of Lincoln. I believe it took its name from the moral darkness, which reigned over that portion of the county, at the time of which I am speaking. If in this point of view, it was but a shade darker than the rest of the county, it was inconceivably dark. If any man can name a trick, or sin, which had not been committed at the time of which I am speaking, in the very focus of all the county's illumination, (Lincolnton) he must himself be the most inventive of the tricky, and the very Judas of sinners. Since that time, however, (all humor aside) Lincoln has become a living proof "that light shineth in darkness." Could I venture to mingle the solemn with the ludicrous, even for the purposes of honorable contrast, I could adduce from this county instances of the most numerous and wonderful transitions, from vice and folly, to virtue and holiness, which have ever perhaps been witnessed since the days of the apostolic ministry. So much, lest it should be thought by some, that what I am about to relate, is characteristic of the county in which it occurred.

3

Whatever may be said of the *moral* condition of the Dark Corner, at the time just mentioned, its *natural* condition was any thing but dark. It smiled in all the charms of spring; and spring borrowed a new charm from its undulating grounds, its luxuriant woodlands, its sportive streams, its vocal birds, and its blushing flowers.

Rapt with the enchantment of the season, and the scenery around me, I was slowly rising the slope, when I was startled by loud, profane and boisterous voices, which seemed to proceed from a thick covert of undergrowth, about two hundred yards in the advance of me, and about one hundred to the right of my road.

"You kin, kin you?"

"Yes, I kin, and am able to do it! Boo-oo-oo! Oh, wake snakes, and walk your chalks! Brimstone and ——— fire! Don't hold me, Nick Stoval! The fight's made up and let's go at it. ——— my soul, if I don't jump down his throat and gallop every chitterling out of him, before you can say 'quit'!"

"Now, Nick, don't hold him! Jist let the wild-cat come, and I'll tame him. Ned 'll see me a fair fight—won't you, Ned?"

"Oh, yes; I'll see you a fair fight, blast my old shoes if I don't."

"That's sufficient, as Tom Haynes said when he saw the Elephant. Now let him come."

Thus they went on, with countless oaths interspersed, which I dare not even hint at, and with much that I could not distinctly hear.

In Mercy's name! thought I, what band of ruffians has selected this holy season, and this heavenly retreat, for such

Pandæmonian riots! I quickened my gait, and had come nearly opposite to the thick grove whence the noise proceeded, when my eye caught indistinctly, and at intervals, through the foliage of the dwarf-oaks and hickories which intervened, glimpses of a man, or men, who seemed to be in a violent struggle; and I could occasionally catch those deep drawn, emphatic oaths, which men in conflict utter, when they deal blows. I dismounted, and hurried to the spot with all speed. I had overcome about half the space which separated it from me, when I saw the combatants come to the ground, and after a short struggle, I saw the uppermost one (for I could not see the other) make a heavy plunge with both his thumbs, and at the same instant I heard a cry in the accent of keenest torture, "Enough! My eye's out!"

A Lincoln Rehearsal

I was so completely horror-struck, that I stood transfixed for a moment to the spot where the cry met me. The accomplices in the hellish deed which had been perpetrated, had all fled at my approach—at least I supposed so, for they were not to be seen.

"Now, blast your corn-shucking soul," said the victor, (a youth about eighteen years old) as he rose from the ground, "come cutt'n your shines 'bout me agin, next time I come to the Court-House, will you! Get your owl-eye in agin if you can!"

At this moment he saw me for the first time. He looked excessively embarrassed, and was moving off, when I called to him, in a tone, emboldened by the sacredness of my office, and the iniquity of his crime, "Come back, you brute! and assist me in relieving your fellow mortal, whom you have ruined forever!"

My rudeness subdued his embarrassment in an instant; and with a taunting curl of the nose, he replied, "You need n't kick before you're spur'd. There a'nt nobody there, nor ha'nt been nother. I was jist seein' how I could 'a' *fout*." So saying, he bounded to his plough, which stood in the corner of the fence about fifty yards beyond the battle ground.

And would you believe it, gentle reader! his report was true. All that I had heard and seen, was nothing more nor less than a Lincoln rehearsal; in which the youth who had just left me, had played all the parts, of all the characters, in a Court-House fight.

I went to the ground from which he had risen; and there were the prints of his two thumbs, plunged up to the balls in the mellow earth, about the distance of a man's eyes apart; and the ground around was broken up, as if two Stags had been engaged upon it.

HALL.

THE DANCE.

A PERSONAL ADVENTURE OF THE AUTHOR.

SOME years ago, I was called by business to one of the frontier counties, then but recently settled. It became necessary for me, while there, to enlist the services of Thomas Gibson, Esq., one of the magistrates of the county, who resided about a mile and a half from my lodgings; and to this circumstance was I indebted for my introduction to him. I had made the intended disposition of my business, and was on the eve of my departure to the city of my residence, when I was induced to remain a day longer, by an invitation from the Squire, to attend a dance at his house on the following day. Having learned from my landlord that I would probably "be expected at the frolick" about the hour of 10 in the forenoon, and being desirous of seeing all that passed upon the occasion, I went over about an hour before the time.

The Squire's dwelling consisted of but one room; which answered the three-fold purpose, of dining room, bed room, and kitchen. The house was constructed of logs, and the floor was of *puncheons*—a term, which in Georgia, means split logs, with their faces a little smoothed with the axe or hatchet. To gratify his daughters, Polly and Silvy, the old gentleman and his lady, had consented to *camp out* for a day, and to surrender the habitation to the girls and their young friends.

When I reached there, I found all things in readiness for the promised amusement. The girls, as the old gentleman informed me, had compelled the family to breakfast under the trees, for they had completely stript the house of its furniture before the sun rose. They were already attired for the dance, in neat, but plain habiliments, of their own manufacture. "What!" says some weakly, sickly, delicate, useless, affected, "charming creature," of the city, "dressed for a Ball at 9 in the morning!" Even so, my delectable Miss Octavia Matilda Juliana Claudia Ipecacuanha: and what have you to say against it? If people must dance, is it not much more rational, to employ the hour allotted to exercise in that amusement, than the hours sacred to repose and meditation? And which is entitled to the most credit; the young lady who rises with the dawn, and puts herself and whole house in order for a Ball, four hours before it begins; or the one who requires a fortnight to get herself dressed for it?

The Squire and I employed the interval in conversation about the first settlement of the country; in the course of which, I picked up some useful, and much interesting information. We were at length interrupted, however, by the sound of a violin, which proceeded from a thick wood at my left. The performer soon after made his appearance, and proved to be no other than Billy Porter, a negro fellow of much harmless wit and humor, who was well known throughout the State. Poor Billy! "his harp is now hung upon the willow"—and I would not blush to offer a tear to his memory, for his name is associated with some of the happiest scenes of my life, and he sleeps with many a dear friend, who used to join me in provoking his wit, and in laughing at his excentricities—but I am leading my reader to the grave, instead of the dance, which I promised. If, however, his memory reaches twelve years back, he will excuse this short tribute of respect to BILLY PORTER.

Billy, to give his own account of himself, "had been taking a turn with the brethren, (the Bar); and hearing the ladies wanted to see *pretty Billy*, had come to give them a benefit." The Squire had not seen him before; and it is no disrespect to his understanding or politeness, to say, that he found it impossible to give me his attention for half an hour after Billy arrived. I had nothing to do, therefore, while the young people were assembling, but to improve my knowledge of Billy's character, to the Squire's amusement. I had been thus engaged about thirty minutes, when I saw several fine, bouncing, ruddy cheeked girls, descending a hill, about the eighth of a mile off. They, too, were attired in manufactures of their own hands. The refinements of the present day in female dress, had not even reached our republican *cities* at this time; and of course, the *country girls* were wholly ignorant of them. They carried no more cloth upon their arms, or straw upon their heads, than was necessary to cover them. They used no artificial means of spreading their frock tails, to an interesting extent from their ankles. They had no boards laced to their breasts, nor any corsets laced to their sides; consequently, they looked, for all the world, like human beings, and could be distinctly recognized as such, at the distance of two hundred paces. Their movements were as free and active, as nature would permit them to be. Let me not be understood, as interposing the least objection, to any lady in this land of liberty, dressing just as she pleases. If she choose to lay her neck and shoulders bare, what right have I to look at them? much less to find fault with them. If she choose to put three yards of muslin in a frock sleeve; what right have I to ask, why a little strip of it, was not put in the body? If she like the pattern of a hoisted umbrella for a frock, and the shape of a cheese-cask for her body; what is all that to me? But to return.

The girls were met by Polly and Silvy Gibson, at some distance from the house; who welcomed them—"with a kiss, of course"—Oh, no; but with something much less equivocal: a hearty shake of the hand and smiling countenances, which had some meaning.

[*Note.*—The custom of kissing, as practised in these days by the *amiables*, is borrowed from the French; and by them from Judas.]

The young ladies had generally collected before any of the young men appeared. It was not long, however, before a large number of both sexes were assembled; and they adjourned to the *Ball room*.

But for the snapping of a fiddle string, the young people would have been engaged in the amusement of the day, in less than three minutes from the time they entered the house. Here, were no formal introductions to be given, no drawing for places or partners, no parade of managers, no ceremonies. It was perfectly understood that all were invited *to dance*, and that none were invited who were unworthy to be danced with; consequently, no gentleman hesitated to ask any lady present to dance with him, and no lady refused to dance with a gentleman, merely because she had not been made acquainted with him.

In a short time the string was repaired, and off went the party to a good old republican six reel. I had been thrown among *fashionables* so long, that I had almost forgotten my native dance. But it revived rapidly as they wheeled through its mazes; and with it returned, many long forgotten, pleasing recollections. Not only did the reel return to me, but the very persons who used to figure in it with me, in the hey-day of youth.

Here was my old sweet-heart, Polly Jackson, identically personified in Polly Gibson; and here was Jim Johnson's, in Silvy; and Bill Martin's, in Nancy Ware. Polly Gibson had my old flame's very steps as well as her looks. "Ah!" said I, "Squire, this puts me in mind of old times. I have not seen a six reel for five and twenty years. It recalls to my mind many a happy hour, and many a jovial friend, who used to enliven it with me. Your Polly, looks so much like my old sweet-heart, Polly Jackson, that were I young again, I certainly should fall in love with her." "That was the name of her mother," said the Squire. "Where did you marry her?" enquired I. "In Wilkes," said he—"she was the daughter of old Nathan Jackson of that county." "It is n't possible!" returned I. Then it is the very girl of whom I am speaking. "Where is she?" "She's out," said the Squire, "preparing dinner for the young people; but she'll be in towards the close of the day. But come along, and I'll make you acquainted with her at once, if you'll promise not to run away with her, for I tell you what it is, she's the likeliest *gal* in all these parts, yet." "Well," said I, "I'll promise not to run away with her, but you must not let her know who I am. I wish to make myself known to her; and for fear of the worst, you shall witness the introduction. But don't get jealous, Squire, if she seems a little too glad to see me; for I assure you, we had a strong notion of each other, when we were young." "No danger," replied the Squire, "she had n't seen *me* then, or she never could have loved such a hard favored man as you are."

In the mean time the dance went on, and I employed myself in selecting from the party, the best examples of the dancers of my day and Mrs. Gibson's, for her entertainment. In this, I had not the least difficulty; for the dancers before me, and those of my day, were in all respects identical.

Jim Johnson kept up the double shuffle from the beginning to the end of the reel: and here was Jim over again in Sammy Tant. Bill Martin always set to his partner with the same step—and a very curious step it was.—He brought his right foot close behind his left, and with it performed precisely the motion of the thumb in cracking that insect which Burns has immortalized; then moved his right back, threw his weight upon it, brought his left behind it, and *cracked* with that as before; and so on alternately. Just so did Bill Kemp, to a nail. Bob Simons danced for all the world like a "Suple Jack," (or as we commonly call it, a *"Suple* Sawney,") when the string is pulled with varied force, at intervals of seconds: and so did *Jake* Slack. Davy Moore, went like a suit of clothes upon a clothing line on a windy day: and here was his antitype in Ned Clarke. Rhoda Nobles swam through the reel like a cork on wavy waters; always giving two or three pretty little perch-bite *diddles,* as she rose from a coupee—Nancy Ware was her very self. Becky Lewis made a business of dancing; she disposed of her part as quick as possible, stopt dead short as soon as she got through, and looked as sober as a Judge all the time—Even so did Chloe Dawson. I used to tell Polly Jackson, that Becky's countenance, when she closed a dance, always seemed to say, "now if you want any more dancing, you may do it yourself."

The dance grew merrier as it progressed; the young people became more easy in each other's company, and often enlivened the scene with most humorous remarks. Occasionally some sharp cuts passed between the boys; such as would have produced a half dozen duels at a city ball; but here they were taken as they were meant, in good humor. Jim Johnson being a little tardy in meeting his partner at a turn of the reel, "I *ax* pardon Miss Chloe," said he, "Jake Slack went to make a crosshop just now, and 'tied his legs in a hard knot, and I stopt to help him untie them." A little after, Jake hung his toe in a crack of the floor, and nearly fell; "Ding my buttons," said he, "if I did'nt know I should stumble over Jim Johnson's foot at last; Jim, draw your foot up to your end of the reel." (Jim was at the other end of the reel, and had in truth a prodigious foot.)

Towards the middle of the day, many of the neighboring farmers dropped in, and joined the Squire and myself in talking of old times. At length dinner was announced. It consisted of plain *fare*, but there was a profusion of it. Rough planks, supported by stakes driven in the ground, served for a table; at which the old and young of both sexes seated themselves at the same time. I soon recognized Mrs. Gibson from all the matrons present. Thirty years had wrought great changes in her appearance; but they had left some of her features entirely unimpaired. Her eye beamed with all its youthful fire; and to my astonishment, her mouth was still beautified with a full set of teeth, unblemished by time. The rose on her cheek had rather freshened than faded, and her smile was the very same that first subdued my heart;

but her fine form was wholly lost; and with it, all the grace
of her movements. Pleasing, but melancholy reflections occupied my mind, as I gazed on her, dispensing her cheerful
hospitalities. I thought of the sad history of many of her
companions and mine, who used to carry light hearts
through the merry dance. I compared my after life with the
cloudless days of my attachment to Polly. Then, I was light
hearted, gay, contented and happy. I aspired to nothing
but a good name, a good wife, and an easy competency.
The first and last were mine already; and Polly had given
me too many little tokens of her favor, to leave a doubt now,
that the second was at my command. But I was foolishly
told, that my talents were of too high an order to be employed in the drudgeries of a farm, and I more foolishly believed it. I forsook the pleasures which I had tried and
proved, and went in pursuit of those imaginary joys, which
seemed to encircle the seat of Fame. From that moment to
the present, my life had been little else than one unbroken
scene of disaster, disappointment, vexation and toil. And
now, when I was too old to enjoy the pleasures which I had
discarded, I found that my aim was absolutely hopeless;
and that my pursuits had only served to unfit me for the
humbler walks of life, and to exclude me from the higher.
The gloom of these reflections was, however, lighted in a
measure, by the promises of the coming hour, when I was to
live over again with Mrs. Gibson, some of the happiest moments of my life.

After a hasty repast, the young people returned to their
amusement; followed by myself, with several of the elders of
the company. An hour had scarcely elapsed, before Mrs.
Gibson entered, accompanied by a goodly number of ma-

trons of her own age. This accession to the company produced its usual effects. It raised the tone of conversation a
full octave, and gave it a triple time movement; added
new life to the wit and limbs of the young folks, and set the
old men to cracking jokes.

At length the time arrived for me to surprise and delight
Mrs. Gibson. The young people insisted upon the old folks
taking a reel; and this was just what I had been waiting for;
for after many plans for making the discovery, I had finally
concluded upon that, which I thought would make *her* joy,
general among the company: and that was, to announce
myself, just before leading her to the dance, in a voice audible to most of the assembly. I therefore readily assented to
the proposition of the young folks, as did two others of my
age, and we made to the ladies for our partners. I of course
offered my hand to Mrs. Gibson.

"Come," said I, "Mrs. Gibson, let us try if we can't out
dance these young people."

"Dear me, Sir," said she, "I haven't danced a step these
twenty years."

"Neither have I, but I've resolved to try once more, if
you will join me, just for old time's sake."

"I really cannot think of dancing," said she.

"Well," continued I, (raising my voice to a pretty high
pitch, on purpose to be heard, while my countenance kindled with exultation at the astonishment and delight which
I was about to produce,) "you surely will dance with an old
friend and sweet-heart, who used to dance with you when a
girl."

At this disclosure, her features assumed a vast variety of
expressions; but none of them responded precisely to my ex-

pectation: indeed, some of them were of such an equivocal and alarming character, that I deemed it advisable not to prolong her suspense. I therefore proceeded.

"Have you forgot your old sweet-heart, Abram Baldwin?" "What!" said she, looking more astonished and confused than ever. "Abram Baldwin!" "Abram Baldwin!" "I don't think I ever heard the name before."

"Do you remember Jim Johnson?" said I.

"Oh yes," said she, "mighty well;" her countenance brightening with a smile.

"And Bill Martin?"

"Yes, perfectly well—why, *who* are you?"

Here we were interrupted by one of the gentlemen who had led his partner to the floor, with "come stranger, we're getting mighty tired o' standing." "It won't do for old people that's going to dance, to take up much time in standing; they'll lose all their *spryness*. Don't stand begging Polly Gibson, she never dances; but take my Sal there next to her, she'll run a reel with you, to old Nick's house and back *agin*." No alternative was left me, and therefore I offered my hand to Mrs. Sally—I didn't know who. "Well," thought I, as I moved to my place, "the Squire is pretty secure from jealousy; but Polly will soon remember me when she sees my steps in the reel. I will dance precisely as I used to in my youth, if it tire me to death. There was one step that was almost exclusively my own, for few of the dancers of my day could perform it at all, and none with the grace and ease that I did. "She'll remember Abram Baldwin," thought I, "as soon as she sees the *double cross-hop*." It was performed by rising and crossing the legs twice or thrice before lighting, and I used to carry it to the third cross with considerable ease. It was a step solely adapted to setting or balancing, as all will perceive; but I thought the occasion would justify a little perversion of it, and therefore resolved to lead off with it, that Polly might be at once relieved from suspense. Just however as I reached my place, Mrs. Gibson's youngest son, a boy about eight years old, ran in and cried out, "Mammy, old Boler's jumpt upon the planks and dragg'd off a great hunk o' meat as big as your head, and broke a dish and two plates all to durn smashes!" Away went Mrs. Gibson, and at the same instant, off went the music. Still I hoped that matters would be adjusted in time for Polly to return and see the double cross hop; and I felt the mortification which my delay in getting a partner had occasioned, somewhat solaced by the reflection, that it had thrown me at the foot of the reel.

The first and second couples had nearly completed their performances, and Polly had not returned. I began to grow uneasy and to interpose as many delays as I could, without attracting notice.

The six reel is closed by the foot couple balancing at the head of the set—then in the middle—then at the foot—again in the middle—meeting at the head, and leading down.

My partner and I had commenced balancing at the head —and Polly had not returned. I balanced until my partner forced me on. I now deemed it advisable to give myself up wholly to the double cross hop; so that if Polly should return in time to see any step, it should be this; though I was already nearly exhausted. Accordingly I made the attempt to introduce it in the turns of the reel; but the first experiment convinced me of three things at once—1st. That I

could not have used the step in this way in my best days—
2d. That my strength would not more than support it in its
proper place for the remainder of the reel, and—3d. If I
tried it again in this way, I should knock my brains out
against the puncheons; for my partner who seemed determined to confirm her husband's report of her, evinced no
disposition to wait upon experiments; but fetching me a jirk
while I was up, and my legs crossed, had well nigh sent me
head foremost to Old Nick's house, sure enough.

We met in the middle, my back to the door, and from the
silence that prevailed in the yard, I flattered myself that
Polly might be even now catching the first glimpse of the
favorite step, when I heard her voice at some distance from
the house—"Get you gone!" "G-e-e-e-t you gone!" "G-e-e-
e-e-e-t you gone!" Matters out doors were now clearly explained. There had been a struggle to get the meat from
Boler—Boler had triumphed, and retreated to the woods
with his booty, and Mrs. Gibson was heaping indignities
upon him in the last resort.

The three *"Get-you-gones"* met me precisely at the three
closing balances; and the last, brought my moral energies to
a perfect level with my physical.

Mrs. Gibson returned, however, in a few minutes after,
in a good humor; for she possessed a lovely disposition,
which even marriage could not spoil. As soon as I could collect breath enough for regular conversation (for to speak in
my native dialect, I was *"mortal tired"*) I took a seat by her,
resolved not to quit the house without making myself
known to her, if possible.

"How much," said I, "your Polly looks, and dances like
you used to, at her age."

"I've told my old man so a hundred times," said she. "Why, who upon earth are you!"

"Did you ever see two persons dance more alike than Jim Johnson and Sammy Tant?" "Never—Why who can you be!"

"You remember Becky Lewis?" "Yes!"

"Well, look at Chloe Dawson, and you'll see her over again."

"Well, law me! Now I know I must have seen you somewhere; but to save my life I can't tell where—Where did your father live?"

"He died when I was small."

"And where did you use to see me?"

"At your father's, and old Mr. Dawson's, and at Mrs. Barnes', and at Squire Nobles', and many other places."

"Well goodness me! it's mighty strange I can't call you to mind."

I now began to get petulant, and thought it best to leave her.

The dance wound up with the old merry jig; and the company dispersed.

The next day I set out for my residence. I had been at home rather more than two months, when I received the following letter from Squire Gisbon.

"DEAR SIR:—I send you the money collected on the notes you left with me. Since you left here, Polly has been thinking about old times, and she says, to save her life she can't recollect you."

BALDWIN.

THE HORSE SWAP.

URING the session of the Superior Court, in the village of ———, about three weeks ago, when a number of people were collected in the principal street of the village, I observed a young man riding up and down the street, as I supposed, in a violent passion. He galloped this way, then that, and then the other. Spurred his horse to one group of citizens, then to another. Then dashed off at half speed, as if fleeing from danger; and suddenly checking his horse, returned—first in a pace, then in a trot, and then in a canter. While he was performing these various evolutions, he cursed, swore, whooped, screamed, and tossed himself in every attitude which man could assume on horse back. In short, he *cavorted* most magnanimously, (a term which, in our tongue, expresses all that I have described, and a little more) and seemed to be setting all creation at defiance. As I like to see all that is passing, I determined to take a position a little nearer to him, and to ascertain if possible, what it was that affected him so sensibly. Accordingly I approached a crowd before which he had stopt for a moment, and examined it with the strictest scrutiny.—But I could see nothing in it, that seemed to have any thing to do with the cavorter. Every man appeared to be in a good humor, and all minding their own business. Not one so much as noticed the principal figure. Still he went on. After a semicolon pause, which my appearance seemed to produce, (for he eyed me closely as I approached) he fetched a whoop, and swore that "he could out-swap any live man, woman or child, that ever walked these hills, or that ever straddled horse flesh since the days of old daddy Adam." "Stranger," said he to me, "did you ever see the *Yallow Blossom* from Jasper?"

"No," said I, "but I have often heard of him."

"I'm the boy," continued he; "perhaps a *leetle*—jist a *leetle* of the best man, at a horse swap, that ever trod shoe-leather."

I began to feel my situation a little awkward, when I was relieved by a man somewhat advanced in years, who stept up and began to survey the "*Yallow Blossom's*" horse with much apparent interest. This drew the rider's attention, and he turned the conversation from me to the stranger.

"Well, my old coon," said he, "do you want to swap *hosses?*"

"Why, I don't know," replied the stranger; I believe I've got a beast I'd trade with you for that one, if you like him."

"Well, fetch up your nag, my old cock; you're jist the lark I wanted to get hold of. I am perhaps a *leetle*, jist a *leetle*, of the best man at a horse swap, that ever stole *crack-lins* out of his mammy's fat gourd. Where's your *hoss?*"

"I'll bring him presently; but I want to examine your horse a little."

"Oh! look at him," said the Blossom, alighting and hitting him a cut—"look at him. He's the best piece of *hoss* flesh in the thirteen united universal worlds. There's no sort o' mistake in little Bullet. He can pick up miles on his feet and fling 'em behind him as fast as the next man's *hoss*, I don't care where he comes from.—And he can keep at it as long as the Sun can shine without resting."

During this harangue, little Bullet looked as if he under-

Blossom and His Horse Bullet

stood it all, believed it, and was ready at any moment to verify it. He was a horse of goodly countenance, rather expressive of vigilance than fire; though an unnatural appearance of fierceness was thrown into it, by the loss of his ears, which had been cropt pretty close to his head. Nature had done but little for Bullet's head and neck; but he managed, in a great measure, to hide their defects, by bowing perpetually. He had obviously suffered severely for corn; but if his ribs and hip bones had not disclosed the fact, *he* never would have done it; for he was in all respects, as cheerful and happy, as if he commanded all the corn-cribs and fodder stacks in Georgia. His height was about twelve hands; but as his shape partook somewhat of that of the Giraffe, his haunches stood much lower. They were short, straight, peaked and concave. Bullet's tail, however, made amends for all his defects. All that the artist could do to beautify it, had been done; and all that horse could do to compliment the artist, Bullet did. His tail was nicked in superior style, and exhibited the line of beauty in so many directions, that it could not fail to hit the most fastidious taste in some of them. From the root it dropt into a graceful festoon; then rose in a handsome curve; then resumed its first direction; and then mounted suddenly upwards like a cypress knee to a perpendicular of about two and a half inches. The whole had a careless and bewitching inclination to the right. Bullet obviously knew where his beauty lay, and took all occasions to display it to the best advantage. If a stick cracked, or if any one moved suddenly about him, or coughed, or hawked, or spoke a little louder than common, up went Bullet's tail like lightning; and if the *going up* did not please, the *coming down* must of necessity, for it was as different from the other movement, as was its direction. The first, was a bold and rapid flight upward; usually to an angle of forty-five degrees. In this position he kept his interesting appendage, until he satisfied himself that nothing in particular was to be done; when he commenced dropping it by half inches, in second beats—then in triple time—then faster and shorter, and faster and shorter still; until it finally died away imperceptibly into its natural position. If I might compare sights to sounds, I should say, its *settling*, was more like the note of a locust than any thing else in nature.

Either from native sprightliness of disposition, from uncontrollable activity, or from an unconquerable habit of removing flies by the stamping of the feet, Bullet never stood still; but always kept up a gentle fly-scaring movement of his limbs, which was peculiarly interesting.

"I tell you, man," proceeded the Yellow Blossom, "he's the best live hoss that ever trod the grit of Georgia. Bob

Smart knows the hoss. Come here, Bob, and mount this hoss and show Bullet's motions." Here, Bullet bristled up, and looked as if he had been hunting for Bob all day long, and had just found him. Bob sprang on his back. "Boo-oo-oo!" said Bob, with a fluttering noise of the lips; and away went Bullet, as if in a quarter race, with all his beauties spread in handsome style.

"Now fetch him back," said Blossom. Bullet turned and came in pretty much as he went out.

"Now trot him by." Bullet reduced his tail to "*customary*" —sidled to the right and left airily, and exhibited at least three varieties of trot, in the short space of fifty yards.

"Make him pace!" Bob commenced twitching the bridle and kicking at the same time. These inconsistent movements obviously (and most naturally) disconcerted Bullet; for it was impossible for him to learn, from them, whether he was to proceed or stand still. He started to trot—and was told that wouldn't do. He attempted a canter—and was checked again. He stopt—and was urged to go on. Bullet now rushed into the wide field of experiment, and struck out a gait of his own, that completely turned the tables upon his rider, and certainly deserved a patent. It seemed to have derived its elements from the jig, the minuet and the cotillon. If it was not a pace, it certainly had *pace* in it; and no man would venture to call it any thing else; so it passed off to the satisfaction of the owner.

"Walk him!" Bullet was now at home again; and he walked as if money was staked on him.

The stranger, whose name I afterwards learned was Peter Ketch, having examined Bullet to his heart's content, ordered his son Neddy to go and bring up Kit. Neddy soon appeared upon Kit; a well formed sorrel of the middle size, and in good order. His *tout ensemble* threw Bullet entirely in the shade; though a glance was sufficient to satisfy any one, that Bullet had the decided advantage of him in point of intellect.

"Why man," said Blossom, "do you bring such a hoss as that to trade for Bullet? Oh, I see you've no notion of trading."

"Ride him off, Neddy!" said Peter. Kit put off at a handsome lope.

"Trot him back!" Kit came in at a long, sweeping trot, and stopt suddenly at the crowd.

"Well," said Blossom, "let me look at him; may be he'll do to plough."

"Examine him!" said Peter, taking hold of the bridle close to the mouth; "He's nothing but a tacky. He an't as *pretty* a horse as Bullet, I know; but he'll do. Start 'em together for a hundred and fifty *mile;* and if Kit an't twenty mile ahead of him at the coming out, any man may take Kit for nothing. But he's a monstrous mean horse, gentlemen; any man may see that. He's the scariest horse, too, you ever saw. He won't do to hunt on, no how. Stranger, will you let Neddy have your rifle to shoot off him? Lay the rifle between his ears, Neddy, and shoot at the blaze in that stump. Tell me when his head is high enough."

Ned fired, and hit the blaze; and Kit did not move a hair's breadth.

"Neddy, take a couple of sticks and beat on that hogshead at Kit's tail."

Ned made a tremendous rattling; at which *Bullet* took fright, broke his bridle and dashed off in grand style; and would have stopt all farther negotiations, by going home in disgust, had not a traveller arrested him and brought him back; but Kit did not move.

"I tell you, gentlemen," continued Peter, "he's the scariest horse you ever saw. He an't as gentle as Bullet; but he won't do any harm if you watch him. Shall I put him in a cart, gig, or wagon for you, stranger? He'll cut the same capers there he does here. He's a monstrous mean horse."

During all this time, Blossom was examining him with the nicest scrutiny. Having examined his frame and limbs, he now looked at his eyes.

"He's got a curious look out of his eyes," said Blossom.

"Oh yes, sir," said Peter, "just as blind as a bat. Blind horses always have clear eyes. Make a motion at his eyes, if you please, sir."

Blossom did so, and Kit threw up his head rather as if something pricked him under the chin, than as if fearing a blow. Blossom repeated the experiment, and Kit jirked back in considerable astonishment.

"Stone blind, you see, gentlemen," proceeded Peter; "but he's just as good to travel of a dark night as if he had eyes."

"Blame my buttons," said Blossom, "if I like them eyes."

"No," said Peter, "nor I neither. I'd rather have 'em made of diamonds; but they'll do, if they don't show as much white as Bullet's."

"Well," said Blossom, "make a pass at me."

"No," said Peter; "you made the banter; now make your pass."

"Well, I'm never afraid to price my hosses. You must give me twenty-five dollars boot."

"Oh certainly; say fifty, and my saddle and bridle in. Here, Neddy, my son, take away daddy's horse."

"Well," said Blossom, "I've made my pass; now you make yours."

"I'm for short talk in a horse swap; and therefore always tell a gentleman, at once, what I mean to do. You must give me ten dollars."

Blossom swore absolutely, roundly and profanely, that he never would give boot.

"Well," said Peter, "I didn't care about trading; but you cut such high shines, that I thought I'd like to back you out; and I've done it. Gentlemen, you see I've brought him to a hack."

"Come, old man," said Blossom, "I've been joking with you. I begin to think you do want to trade; therefore, give me five dollars and take Bullet. I'd rather lose ten dollars, any time, than not make a trade; though I hate to fling away a good hoss."

"Well," said Peter, "I'll be as clever as you are. Just put the five dollars on Bullet's back and hand him over, it's a trade."

Blossom swore again, as roundly as before, that he would not give boot; and, said he, "Bullet wouldn't hold five dollars on his back, no how. But as I bantered you, if you say an even swap, here's at you."

"I told you," said Peter, "I'd be as clever as you; therefore, here goes two dollars more, just for trade sake. Give three dollars, and it's a bargain."

Blossom repeated his former assertion; and here the parties stood for a long time, and the by-standers (for many were now collected,) began to taunt both parties. After some time, however, it was pretty unanimously decided that the old man had backed Blossom out.

At length Blossom swore he "never would be backed out, for three dollars, after bantering a man;" and accordingly they closed the trade.

"Now," said Blossom, as he handed Peter the three dollars, "I'm a man, that when he makes a bad trade, makes the most of it until he can make a better. I'm for no rues and after-claps."

"That's just my way," said Peter; "I never goes to law to mend my bargains."

"Ah, you're the kind of boy I love to trade with. Here's your hoss, old man. Take the saddle and bridle off him, and I'll strip yours; but lift up the blanket easy from Bullet's back, for he's a mighty tenderbacked hoss."

The old man removed the saddle, but the blanket stuck fast. He attempted to raise it, and Bullet bowed himself, switched his tail, danced a little, and gave signs of biting.

"Don't hurt him, old man," said Blossom archly; "take it off easy. I am, perhaps, a leetle of the best man at a horse-swap that ever catched a coon."

Peter continued to pull at the blanket more and more roughly; and Bullet became more and more *cavortish:* in so much, that when the blanket came off, he had reached the *kicking* point in good earnest.

The removal of the blanket, disclosed a sore on Bullet's back-bone, that seemed to have defied all medical skill. It measured six full inches in length, and four in breadth; and had as many features as Bullet had motions. My heart sickened at the sight; and I felt that the brute who had been riding him in that situation, deserved the halter.

The prevailing feeling, however, was that of mirth. The laugh became loud and general, at the old man's expense; and rustic witticisms were liberally bestowed upon him and his late purchase. These, Blossom continued to provoke by various remarks. He asked the old man, "if he thought Bullet would let five dollars lie on his back." He declared most seriously, that he had owned that horse three months, and had never discovered before, that he had a sore back, "or he never should have thought of trading him," &c. &c.

The old man bore it all with the most philosophic composure. He evinced no astonishment at his late discovery, and made no replies. But his son, Neddy, had not disciplined his feelings quite so well. His eyes opened, wider and wider, from the first to the last pull of the blanket; and when the whole sore burst upon his view, astonishment and fright seemed to contend for the mastery of his countenance. As the blanket disappeared, he stuck his hands in his breeches pockets, heaved a deep sigh, and lapsed into a profound reverie; from which he was only roused by the cuts at his father. He bore them as long as he could; and when he could contain himself no longer, he began, with a certain wildness of expression, which gave a peculiar interest to what he uttered: "His back's mighty bad off; but dod drot my soul, if he's put it to daddy as bad as he thinks he has, for old Kit's both blind and *deef*, I'll be dod drot if he eint."

"The devil he is," said Blossom. "Yes, dod drot my soul if he *eint*. You walk him and see if he *eint*. His eyes don't look like it; but he *jist as live go agin* the house with you, or in a ditch, as any how. Now you go try him." The laugh was now turned on Blossom; and many rushed to test the fidelity of the little boy's report. A few experiments established its truth, beyond controversy.

"Neddy," said the old man, you oughn't to try and make people discontented with their things." "Stranger, don't mind what the little boy says. If you can only get Kit rid of them little failings, you'll find him all sorts of a horse. You are a *leetle* the best man, at a horse swap, that ever I got hold of; but don't fool away Kit. Come, Neddy, my son, let's be moving; the stranger seems to be getting snappish."

HALL.

THE CHARACTER OF A NATIVE GEORGIAN.

THERE are some yet living, who knew the man whose character I am about to delineate; and these will unanimously bear testimony, that if it be not faithfully drawn, it is not overdrawn. They cannot avouch for the truth of the anecdotes which I am about to relate of him, because of these they know nothing; but they will unhesitatingly declare, that there is nothing herein ascribed to him, of which he was incapable, and of which he would not readily have been the author, supposing the scenes in which I have placed him to be real, and the thoughts and actions attributed to him, to have actually suggested themselves to him. They will further testify, that the thoughts and actions, are in perfect harmony with his general character.

I do not feel at liberty as yet to give the name of the person in question, and therefore, he shall be designated for the present, by the appellation of Ned Brace.

This man seemed to live only to amuse himself with his fellow-beings, and he possessed the rare faculty, of deriving some gratification of his favorite propensity, from almost every person with whom he met, no matter what his temper, standing or disposition. Of course he had opportunities enough of exercising his uncommon gift, and he rarely suffered an opportunity to pass unimproved. The beau in the presence of his mistress, the fop, the pedant, the purse-proud, the over-fastidious and sensitive, were Ned's favorite game. These never passed him uninjured; and against such, he directed his severest shafts. With these he commonly amused himself, by exciting in them every variety of emotion, under circumstances peculiarly ridiculous. He was admirably fitted to his vocation. He could assume any character which his humor required him to personate, and he could sustain it to perfection. His knowledge of the character of others, seemed to be intuitive.

It may seem remarkable, but it is true, that though he lived his own peculiar life for about sixteen years, after he reached the age of manhood, he never involved himself in a personal recounter with any one. This was owing in part to his muscular frame, which few would be willing to engage; but more particularly to his adroitness in the management of his projects of fun. He generally conducted them in such a way, as to render it impossible for any one to call him to account, without violating all the rules of decency, politeness and chivalry at once. But a few anecdotes of him, will give the reader a much better idea of his character, than he can possibly derive from a general description. If these fulfil the description which I have given of my hero, all will agree that he is no imaginary being: if they do not, it will only be, because I am unfortunate in my selection. Having known him from his earliest manhood to his grave—for he was a native Georgian—I confess, that I am greatly perplexed, in determining what portions of his singular history, to lay before the reader, as a proper specimen of the whole. A three days' visit, which I once made with him to Savannah, placed him in a greater variety of scenes, and among a greater diversity of characters, than perhaps any other period of his life, embracing no longer time; and therefore, I will choose this for my purpose.

We reached Savannah just at night-fall, of a cold December's evening. As we approached the tavern of Mr. Blank, at which we designed to stop, Ned proposed to me, that we should drop our acquaintance, until *he* should choose to renew it. To this proposition I most cordially assented, for I knew, that so doing, I should be saved some mortifications, and avoid a thousand questions, which I would not know how to answer. According to this understanding, Ned lingered behind, in order that I might reach the tavern alone.

On alighting at the public house, I was led into a large dining-room, at the entrance of which, to the right, stood the bar, opening into the dining-room. On the left, and rather nearer to the centre of the room, was a fire-place, surrounded by gentlemen. Upon entering the room, my name was demanded at the bar: it was given, and I took my seat in the circle around the fire. I had been seated just long enough for the company to survey me to their satisfaction, and resume their conversation, when Ned's heavy footstep at the door, turned the eyes of the company to the approaching stranger.

"Your name sir, if you please?" said the restless little bar-keeper, as he entered.

Ned stared at the question with apparent alarm—cast a fearful glance at the company—frowned and shook his head in token of caution to the bar-keeper—looked confused for a moment—then, as if suddenly recollecting himself, jirked a piece of paper out of his pocket—turned from the company —wrote on it with his pencil—handed it to the bar-keeper —walked to the left of the fire-place, and took the most conspicuous seat in the circle. He looked at no one, spoke to no one; but fixing his eyes on the fire, lapsed into a profound reverie.

The conversation, which had been pretty general before, stopped as short, as if every man in the room had been shot dead. Every eye was fixed on Ned, and every variety of expression was to be seen on the countenances of the persons present. The landlord came in—the bar-keeper whispered to him and looked at Ned. The landlord looked at him too with astonishment and alarm—the bar-keeper produced a piece of paper, and both of them examined it, as if searching for a fig-mite with the naked eye. They rose from the examination unsatisfied, and looked at Ned again. Those of the company who recovered first from their astonishment, tried to revive the conversation; but the effort was awkward, met with no support, and failed. The bar-keeper, for the first time in his life, became dignified and solemn, and left the bar to take care of itself. The landlord had a world of foolish questions to ask the gentlemen directly opposite to Ned, for which purpose he passed round to them every two minutes, and the answer to none did he hear.

Three or four boarders coming in, who were unapprized of what had happened, at length revived the conversation; not however, until they had created some confusion, by enquiring of their friends, the cause of their sober looks. As soon as the conversation began to become easy and natural, Ned rose, and walked out into the entry. With the first movement, all were as hush as death; but when he had cleared the door, another Babel scene ensued. Some enquired, others suspected, and all wondered. Some were engaged in telling the strangers what had happened, others were making towards the bar, and all were becoming clamorous, when Ned returned and took his seat. His re-entry was as fatal to conversation, as was the first movement of his exit; but it soon recovered from the shock—with the difference, however, that those who *led* before, were now mute, and wholly absorbed in the contemplation of Ned's person.

After retaining his seat for about ten minutes, Ned rose again, enquired the way to the stable, and left the house. As soon as he passed the outer door, the bar-keeper hastened to the company with Ned's paper in his hand. "Gentlemen," said he, "can any of you tell me what name this is?" All rushed to the paper in an instant—one or two pair of heads met over it with considerable force. After pondering over it to their heart's content, they all agreed that the first letter was an "E" and the second a "B" or an "R," and the d——l himself could not make out the balance. While they were thus engaged, to the astonishment of every body, Ned interrupted their deliberations with "gentlemen, if you have satisfied yourselves with that paper, I'll thank you for it." It is easy to imagine, but impossible to describe the looks and actions of the company, under their surprise and mortification. They dropt off and left the bar-keeper to his appropriate duty, of handing the paper to Ned. He reached it forth, but Ned moved not a hand to receive it, for about the space of three seconds; during which time he kept his eyes fixed upon the arch-offender in awfully solemn rebuke. He then took it gravely and put it in his pocket, and left the bar-keeper, with a shaking ague upon him. From this moment he became Ned's most obsequious and willing slave.

Supper was announced; Mrs. Blank, the landlady, took the head of the table, and Ned seated himself next to her. Her looks denoted some alarm at finding him so near to her; and plainly showed, that he had been fully described to her by her husband, or some one else.

"Will you take tea or coffee, sir?" said she.

"Why madam," said Ned, in a tone as courteous as Chesterfield himself could have used, "I am really ashamed to acknowledge and to expose my very singular appetite; but habitual indulgence of it, has made it necessary to my comfort, if not to my health, that I should still favor it when I can. If you will pardon me, I will take both at the same time."

This respectful reply, (which, by the way, she alone was permitted to hear,) had its natural effect. It won for him her unqualified indulgence, raised doubts whether he could be the suspicious character which had been described to her, and begat in her a desire to cultivate a further acquaintance with him. She handed to him the two cups, and accompanied them with some remarks drawn from her own

observation in the line of her business, calculated to reconcile him to his whimsical appetite; but she could extract
from Ned nothing but monosyllables, and sometimes not
even that much. Consequently, the good lady began very
soon to relapse into her former feelings.

Ned placed a cup on either side of him, and commenced
stirring both at the same time very deliberately. This done,
he sipped a little tea, and asked Mrs. B. for a drop more
milk in it. Then he tasted his coffee, and desired a little
more sugar in it. Then he tasted his tea again and requested
a small lump more sugar in it—Lastly he tasted his coffee,
and desired a few drops more milk in that. It was easy to
discover, that before he got suited, the landlady had solemnly resolved, never to offer any more encouragements to
such an appetite. She waxed exceedingly petulant, and having nothing else to scold, she scolded the servants of course.

Waffles were handed to Ned, and he took one: batter-
cakes were handed, and he took one; and so on of muffins,
rolls, and corn bread. Having laid in these provisions, he
turned into his plate, upon his waffle and batter-cake, some
of the crumbs of the several kinds of bread which he had
taken, in different proportions, and commenced mashing
all together with his knife. During this operation the landlady frowned and pouted,—the servants giggled,—and the
boarders were variously affected.

Having reduced his mess to the consistency of a hard
poultice, he packed it all up to one side of his plate in the
form of a terrapin, and smoothed it all over nicely with his
knife. Nearly opposite to Ned, but a little below him, sat a
waspish little gentleman, who had been watching him with
increasing torments, from the first to the last movement of

Ned's knife. His tortures were visible to blinder eyes than Ned's, and doubtless had been seen by him in their earliest paroxysms. This gentleman occupied a seat nearest to a dish of steak, and was in the act of muttering something about "brutes" to his next neighbor, when Ned beckoned a servant to him, and requested him "to ask that gentleman for a small bit of steak." The servant obeyed, and planting Ned's plate directly between the gentleman's and the steak-dish, delivered his message. The testy gentleman turned his head, and the first thing he saw was Ned's party-coloured terrapin, right under his nose. He started as if he had been struck by a snapping-turtle—reddened to scarlet—looked at Ned, (who appeared as innocent as a lamb)—looked at the servant, (who appeared as innocent as Ned) and then fell to work on the steak, as if he were amputating all Ned's limbs at once.

Ned now commenced his repast. He ate his meat and *breads* in the usual way; but he drank his liquids in all ways. First a sip of tea, then of coffee; then two of the first and one of the last; then three of the last, and one of the first, and so on.

His steak was soon consumed, and his plate was a second time to the mettlesome gentleman "for another *very* small bit of steak." The plate paid its second visit, precisely as it had its first; and as soon as the fiery gentleman saw the half-demolished terrapin again under his nose, he seized a fork, drove it into the largest slice of steak in the dish, dashed it into Ned's plate, rose from the table, and left the room; cursing Ned from the very inmost chamber of his soul. Every person at the table, except Ned, laughed outright at the little man's fury; but Ned did not even smile—nay, he looked for all the world, as if he thought the laugh was at him.

The boarders, one after another, retired, until Ned and the landlady were left alone at the table.

"Will you have another cup of tea and coffee sir?" said she, by the way of convincing him that he ought to retire, seeing that he had finished his supper.

"No I thank you madam," returned Ned.

"Will you have a glass of milk and a cup of tea or coffee; or all three together?"

"No ma'am," said Ned. "I am not blind madam," continued he, "to the effects which my unfortunate eccentricities have produced upon yourself and your company; nor have I witnessed them without those feelings which they are well calculated to inspire in a man of ordinary sensibilities. I am aware, too, that I am prolonging and aggravating your uneasiness, by detaining you beyond the hour which demands your presence at the table; but I could not permit you to retire, without again bespeaking your indulgence of the strange, unnatural appetite, which has just caused you so much astonishment and mortification. The story of its beginning might be interesting, and certainly would be instructing to you if you are a mother: but I am indisposed at this time to obtrude it upon your patience, and I presume you are still less disposed to hear it. My principal object, however, in claiming your attention for a moment at this time, is to assure you, that out of respect to your feelings, I will surrender the enjoyment of my meals for the few days that I have to remain in Savannah, and conform to the customs of your table. The sudden change of my habits will expose me to some inconvenience, and may perhaps affect my health; but I willingly incur these hazards, rather than to renew your mortification, or to impose upon your family the trouble of giving me my meals at my room."

The good lady, whose bitter feelings had given place to the kinder emotion of pity and benevolence, before Ned had half concluded his apology, (for it was delivered in a tone of the most melting eloquence,) caught at this last hint, and insisted upon sending his meals to his room. Ned reluctantly consented, after extorting a pledge from her, that *she* would assume the responsibilities of the trouble that he was about to give the family.

"As to your *boarders*, madam," said Ned, in conclusion, "I have no apology to make to them. I grant them the privilege of eating what they please, and as they please; and so far as they are concerned I shall exercise the same privileges, reckless of their feelings or opinions; and I shall take it as a singular favor if you will say nothing to them or to any one else, which may lead them to the discovery, that I am acquainted with my own peculiarities."

The good lady promised obedience to his wishes, and Ned, requesting to be conducted to the room, retired.

A group of gentlemen at the fire-place had sent many significant "hems" and smiles to Mrs. Blank, during her *tête à tête* with Ned; and as she approached them, on her way out of the room, they began to taunt her playfully, upon the impression which she seemed to have made upon the remarkable stranger.

"Really," said one, "I thought the *impression* was on the other side."

"And in truth, so it was," said Mrs. B. At this moment her husband stept in.

"I'll tell you what it is, Mr. Blank," said one of the company, "you'd better keep a sharp look out on that stranger; our landlady is wonderfully taken with him."

"I'll be bound," said Mr. B. "for my wife; the less like any body else in the world he is, the better will she like him."

"Well I assure you," said Mrs. B., "I never had my feelings so deeply interested in a stranger in my life. I'd give the world to know his history."

"Why, then," rejoined the landlord; "I suppose he has been quizzing us all this time."

"No," said she, "he is incapable of quizzing. All that you have seen of him is unaffected, and perfectly natural to him."

"Then, really," continued the husband, "he is a very interesting object, and I congratulate you upon getting so early into his confidence; but as I am not quite as much captivated with his unaffected graces as you seem to be, I shall take the liberty, in charity to the rest of my boarders, of requesting him to-morrow, to seek other lodgings."

"Oh," exclaimed Mrs. B. in the goodness of her heart, and with a countenance evincive of the deepest feeling, "I would not have you do such a thing for the world. He's only going to stay a few days."

"How do you know?"

"He told me so, and do let's bear with him that short time. He sha'nt trouble you or the boarders any more."

"Why Sarah," said the landlord, "I do believe you are out of your senses!"

"Gone case!" said one boarder. "Terrible affair!" said another. "Bewitching *little* fellow," said a third. "Come,

Mrs. Blank, tell us all he said to you? We young men wish to know how to please the ladies, so that we may get wives easily. I'm determined the next party I go to, to make a soup of everything on the waiters, and eat all at once. I shall then become irresistible to the ladies."

"Get along with your nonsense," said Mrs. B. smiling as she left the room.

At 8 o'clock, I retired to my room, which happened (probably from the circumstance of our reaching the hotel within a few minutes of each other,) to be adjoining Ned's. I had no sooner entered my room, than Ned followed me, where we interchanged the particulars which make up the foregoing story. He now expended freely the laughter which he had been collecting during the evening. He stated that his last interview with Mrs. Blank, was the result of neces- sity—That he found he had committed himself in making up and disposing of his odd supper; for that he should have to eat in the same way, during his whole stay in Savannah, unless he could manage to get his meals in private; and though he was willing to do penance for one meal, in order to purchase the amusement which he had enjoyed, he had no idea of tormenting himself three or four days for the same purpose. To tell you the honest truth, said he, nothing but an appetite whetted by fasting and travelling, could have borne me through the table scene. As it was, my stom- ach several times threatened to expose my tricks to the whole company, by downright open rebellion. I feel that I must make it some atonement for the liberty I have taken with it; and therefore, propose that we go out and get an oyster supper before we retire to rest. I assented: we set out, going separately, until we reached the street.

We were received by the oyster-vender, in a small shop, which fronted upon the street, and were conducted through it to a back door, and thence, by a flight of steps, to a convenient room, on a second floor of an adjoining building. We had been seated about three minutes, when we heard footsteps on the stairs, and distinctly caught this sentence from the ascending stranger: "Aha, Monsieur Middletong! you say you hab de bes oystar in de cittee? Well, me shall soon see."

The sentence was hardly uttered, before the door opened, and in stept a gay, smerky little Frenchman. He made us a low bow, and as soon as he rose from his obeisance, Ned rushed to him in transports of joy—seized him by the hand, and shaking it with friendship's warmest grasp, exclaimed, "How do you do my old friend—I had no idea of meeting you here—how do you do Mr. Squeezelfanter? how have you been this long time?"

"Sair," said the Frenchman, "me tank you ver' much to lub me so hard; but you mistake de gentleman—my name is not de Squeezilfaunter."

"Come, come John," continued Ned, "quit your old tricks before strangers. Mr. Hall, let me introduce you to my particular friend, John Squeezelfanter, from Paris."

"Perhaps, sir," said I—not knowing well what to say, or how to act in such an emergency—"perhaps you have mistaken the gentleman."

"Begar, sair," said Monsieur, "he is mistake ebery ting at once. My name is not *Zhaun*, me play no *treek*, me is not de gentilmong fren', me did not come from *Paree*, but from Bordeaux—and me did not suppose dare was one man in all France, dat was name de Squeezilfaunter."

"If I am mistaken," said Ned, "I humbly ask your pardon; but really, you look so much like my old friend *Jack*, and talk so much like him, that I would have sworn you were he."

"Vell, sair," said Monsieur, looking at Ned as though he might be an acquaintance after all—"vell, sair, dis time you tell my name right—my name is Jacques*—*Jacques Sancric.*

"There," proceeded Ned, "I knew it was impossible I could be mistaken—your whole family settled on *Sandy Creek*—I knew your father and mother, your sister Patsy and Dilsy, your brother Ichabod, your aunt Bridget, your —— —."

"Oh mon Dieu, mon Dieu!" exclaimed the Frenchman, no longer able to contain his surprise; "dat is von 'Mericane familee. Dare vas not one French familee hab all dat name since dis vorl' vas make."

"Now look at me good Jack," said Ned, "and see if you don't recollect your old friend Obadiah Snoddleburg, who used to play with you when a boy, in Sandy Creek."

"Vell, Monsieur Snotborg, me look at you ver' well; and begar me neber see you in de creek, nor out de creek—'Tis ver' surprise, you not know one *name*, from one *creek*."

"Oh, very well sir, very well, I forgot where I was—I understand you now perfectly. You are not the first gentleman I have met with in Savannah, who knew me well in the country, and forgot me in town. I ask your pardon sir, and hope you'll excuse me."

"Me is ver' will to know you *now*, sair; but begar me will not tell you one lie, to know you *twenty-five and tirty years ago.*"

"It makes no difference sir," said Ned, looking thought-

* This name in French is pronounced very nearly like " Jack," in English.

fully and chagrined. "I beg leave, however, before we close our acquaintance; to correct one mistake which I made.—I said you were from Paris—I believe on reflection, I was wrong—I think your sister Dilsy told me you *were* from Bordeaux."

"Foutre, de sist, Dils!—Here Monsieur Middletong! My oystar ready?"

"Yes sir."

"Vell, if my oystar ready, you give dem to my fren' Monsieur Snotborg; and ask him to be so good to carry dem to my sist' Dils, and my brodder Ichbod on Sand' Creek."—So saying, he vanished like lightning.

The next morning at breakfast, I occupied Ned's seat. Mrs. Blank had no sooner taken her place, than she ordered a servant to bring her a waiter; upon which she placed a cup of tea, and another of coffee—then ordering three plates, she placed them on it; sent one servant for one kind of bread, and another for another, and so on through all the varieties that were on the table, from which she made selections for plate No. 1. In the same way did she collect meats for plate No. 2—No. 3 she left blank. She had nearly completed her operations, when her husband came to know why every servant was engaged, and no gentleman helped to any thing, when the oddly furnished waiter met his eye, and fully explained the wonder.

"In God's name, Sarah," said he, "who are you mixing up those messes for?"

"For that strange gentleman we were speaking of last night," was the reply.

"Why doesn't he come to the table?"

"He was very anxious to come, but I would not let him."

"*You* would not let him! Why not?"

"Because I did not wish to see a man of his delicate sensibilities ridiculed and insulted at my table."

"Delicate devilabilities! Then why did'nt you send a *servant* to collect his mixtures?"

"Because I preferred doing it myself, to troubling the boarders. I knew that wherever his plates went, the gentlemen would be making merry over them, and I could'nt bear to see it."

The landlord looked at her for a moment, with commingled astonishment, doubt, and alarm; and then upon the breath of a deep drawn sigh proceeded.—

"Well, d——n* the man! He has'nt been in the house more than two hours, except when he was asleep, and he has insulted one half my boarders, made fools of the other half, turned the head of my bar-keeper, crazed all my servants, and run my wife right stark, staring, raving mad—A man who is a perfect clown in his manners, and who, I have no doubt, will, in the end, prove to be a horse thief."

Much occurred between the landlord and his lady in relation to Ned, which we must of necessity omit. Suffice it to say, that her assiduities to Ned, her unexplained sympathies for him, her often repeated desires to become better acquainted with him, conspiring with one or two short interviews which her husband saw between her and Ned, (and which consisted of nothing more than expressions of regret on his part, at the trouble he was giving the family, and assurance on hers, that it was no trouble at all,) began to

* I should certainly omit such expressions as this, could I do so with historic fidelity; but the peculiarities of the times of which I am writing, cannot be faithfully represented without them. In recording things *as they are*, truth requires me sometimes to put profane language into the mouths of my characters.

bring upon the landlord, the husband's worst calamity. This she soon observed, and considering her duty to her husband as of paramount obligation, she gave him an explanation that was entirely satisfactory. She told him that Ned was a man of refined feelings and high cultivated mind, but that in his infancy his mother had forced him to eat different kinds of diet together, until she had produced in him a vitiated and unconquerable appetite, which he was now constrained to indulge, as the drunkard does his, or be miserable. As the good man was prepared to believe any story of *woman's* folly, he was satisfied.

This being the Sabbath, at the usual hour, Ned went to Church, and selected for his morning's service, one of those Churches in which the pews are free, and in which the hymn is given out, and sung by the congregation, a half recitative.

Ned entered the Church, in as fast a walk as he could possibly assume—proceeded about half down the aisle, and popt himself down in his seat as quick as if he had been shot. The more thoughtless of the congregation began to titter, and the graver peeped up slily, but solemnly at him.

The Pastor rose, and before giving out the hymn, observed, that *singing* was a part of the service, in which he thought the whole congregation ought to join. Thus saying, he gave out the first lines of the hymn. As soon as the tune was raised, Ned struck in, with one of the loudest, hoarsest, most discordant voices, that ever annoyed a solemn assembly.

"I would observe," said the preacher, before giving out the next two lines, "that there are some persons who have not the gift of singing; such of course are not expected to

sing." Ned took the hint, and sang no more; but his entrance into church, and his entrance into the hymn, had already dispersed the solemnity of three fifths of the congregation.

Ned Brace at Church

As soon as the Pastor commenced his sermon, Ned opened
his eyes, threw back his head, dropt his underjaw, and surrendered himself to the most intense interest. The preacher
was an indifferent one, and by as much as he became dull
and insipid, by so much did Ned become absorbed in the
discourse. And yet it was impossible for the nicest observer
to detect any thing in his looks or manner, short of the most
solemn devotion. The effect which his conduct had upon
the congregation, and their subsequent remarks must be
left to the imagination of the reader. I give but one remark
—"Bless that good man who came in the Church so quick,"
said a venerable matron as she left the church door, "how
he was affected by the *sarment*."

Ned went to church no more on that day. About four

o'clock in the afternoon, while he was standing at the tavern door, a funeral procession passed by, at the foot of which, and singly, walked one of the smallest men I ever saw. As soon as he came opposite the door, Ned stept out and joined him with great solemnity. The contrast between the two was ludicrously striking, and the little man's looks and uneasiness, plainly showed that he felt it. However, he soon became reconciled to it. They proceeded but a little way before Ned enquired of his companion, who was dead?

Ned Brace and the Little Man at a Funeral

"Mr. Noah Bills," said the little man.

"Nan?" said Ned, raising his hand to his ear in token of deafness, and bending his head to the speaker.

"Mr. Noah Bills," repeated the little man loud enough to disturb the two couples immediately before him.

"Mrs. Noel's Bill!" said Ned, with mortification and astonishment. "Do the white persons pay such respect to niggers in Savannah? *I* sha'nt do it"—So saying he left the procession.

The little man was at first considerably nettled; but upon being left to his own reflections, he got into an uncontrollable fit of laughter, as did the couple immediately in advance of him, who overheard Ned's remark. The procession now exhibited a most mortifying spectacle—The head of it in mourning and in tears, and the foot of it convulsed with laughter.

On Monday, Ned employed himself in disposing of the business which brought him to Savannah, and I saw but little of him; but I could not step into the street without hearing of him. All talked about him, and hardly any two agreed about his character.

On Tuesday he visited the Market, and set it all in astonishment or laughter. He wanted to buy something of every body, and some of every thing; but could not agree upon the terms of a trade, because he always wanted his articles in such portions and numbers, as no one would sell, or upon conditions to which no one would submit. To give a single example—He beset an old negro woman to sell him the half of a living chicken.

"Do my good mauma, sell it to me," said he, "my wife is very sick, and is longing for chicken pie, and this is all the money I have," (holding out twelve and a half cents in silver,) "and it's just what a half chicken comes to at your own price."

"Ki, massa! How gwine cut live chicken in two?"

"I don't want you to cut it in two alive—kill it, clean it, and then divide it."

"Name o' God! What sort o' chance got to clean chicken in de market-house!—Whay de water for scall um, and wash um?"

"Don't scald it at all; just pick it so."

"Ech-ech! Fedder fly all ober de buckera-man meat, he come bang me fo' true—No massa, I mighty sorry for your wife, but I no cutty chicken open."

In the afternoon, Ned entered the dining room of the tavern, and who should he find there but Monsieur Sancric, of oyster-house memory. He and the tavern-keeper were alone. With the first glimpse of Ned, "La diable," exclaimed the Frenchman, "here my broder Ichbod gain!"—and away he went.

"Mr. Sancric!" said the landlord, calling to him as if to tell him something just thought of, and following him out, "What did you say that man's name is?"

"He name Monsieur Snotborg."

"Why that can't be his name, for it begins with a B or an R. Where is he from?"

"From Sand Creek."

"Where did you know him?"

"Begar, me neber did know him." Here Ned sauntered in sight of the Frenchman, and he vanished.

"Well," said the landlord, as he returned, "it does seem to me, that every body who has anything to do with that man, runs crazy forthwith."

When he entered the dining room he found Ned deeply engaged reading a child's primer, with which he seemed wonderfully delighted. The landlord sat for a moment, smiled, and then hastily left the room. As soon as he disappeared, Ned laid down his book, and took his station behind some cloaks in the bar, which at the moment was deserted. He had just reached his place, when the landlord returned with his lady.

"Oh," said the first, "he's gone! I brought you in to show you what kind of books your man of 'refined feelings and highly cultivated mind' delights in—But he has left his book, and here it is, opened at the place where he left off—and do let's see what's in it?"

They examined, and found that he had been reading the interesting poem of 'Little Jack Horner.'

"Now," continued the landlord, "if you'll believe me, he was just as much delighted with that story, as you or I would be with the best written number of the Spectator."

"Well, it's very strange," said Mrs. Blank—"I reckon he must be flighty, for no man could have made a more gentlemanly apology than he did to me, for his peculiarities; and no one could have urged it more feelingly."

"One thing is very certain," said the husband, "if he be not flighty himself, he has a wonderful knack of making every body else so. Sancric ran away from him just now, as if he had seen the devil—called him by one name when he left the room, by another at the door, told me where he came from, and finally swore he did not know him at all."

Ned having slipt softly from the bar into the entry, during this interview, entered the dining room, as if from the street.

"I am happy," said he, smiling, "to meet you together and alone, upon the eve of my departure from Savannah, that I may explain to you my singular conduct, and ask your forgiveness of it. I will do so if you will not expose my true character until I shall have left the city."

This they promised—"My name then," continued he, "is Edward Brace, of Richmond county. Humor has been my besetting sin from my youth, up. It has sunk me far below the station to which my native gifts entitled me. It has robbed me of the respect of all my acquaintances; and what is much more to be regretted, the esteem of some of my best and most indulgent friends. All this I have long known, and I have a thousand times deplored, and as often resolved to conquer, my self-destroying propensity. But so deeply is it wrought into my very nature—so completely and indissolubly interwoven is it, with every fibre and filament of my being, that I have found it impossible for me to subdue it. Being on my first visit to Savannah, unknowing and unknown, I could not forego the opportunity which it furnished, of gratifying my ungovernable proclivity. All the extravagancies which you have seen, have been in subservience to it."

He then explained the cause of his troubling the kind lady before him, to give him his meals at his room, and the strange conduct of Monsieur Sancric; at which they both laughed heartily. He referred them to me for confirmation of what he had told them. Having gone thus far, continued he, "I must sustain my character until to-morrow, when I shall leave Savannah."

Having now two more to enjoy his humor with him and myself, he let himself loose that night among the boarders, with all his strength, and never did I see two mortals laugh, as did Mr. and Mrs. Blank.

Far as I have extended this sketch, I cannot close, without exhibiting Ned in one new scene, in which accident placed him before he left Savannah.

About 2 o'clock on the morning of our departure, the town was alarmed by the cry of fire. Ned got up before me, and taking one of my boots from the door, and putting one of his in its place, he marched down to the front door with odd boots. On coming out and finding what had been done, I knew that Ned could not have left the house, for it was impossible for him to wear my boot. I was about descending the stairs, when he called to me from the front door, and said the servant had mixed our boots, and that he had brought down one of mine. When I reached the front door, I found Ned and Mr. and Mrs. Blank there; all the inmates of the house having left it, who designed to leave it, but Ned and myself.

"Don't go and leave me Hall," said he, holding my boot in his hand, and having his own on his leg.

"How can I leave you," said I, "unless you'll give me my boot?" This he did not seem to hear.

"Do run gentlemen," said Mrs. Blank greatly alarmed— "Mr. Brace, you've got Mr. Hall's boot, give it to him."

"In a minute madam," said he, seeming to be beside himself. A second after, however, all was explained to me. He designed to have my company to the fire, and his own fun before he went.

A man came posting along in great alarm, and crying "fire" loudly. "Mister, Mister," said Ned, jumping out of the house.

"Sir," said the man, stopping and puffing awfully.

"Have you seen Mr. Peleg Q. C. Stone," along where you've been?" enquired Ned, with anxious solicitude.

"D—n Mr. Peleg Q. C. Stone," said the stranger,— "What chance have I of seeing any body, hopping up at two o'clock in the morning, and the town a fire!" and on he went.

Thus did he amuse himself with various questions and remarks, to four or five passengers, until even Mrs. Blank forgot for a while, that the town was in flames. The last object of his sport, was a woman who came along, exclaiming, "Oh, it's Mr. Dalby's house—I'm sure it is Mr. Dalby's house!" Two gentlemen assured her, that the fire was far beyond Mr. Dalby's house; but still she went on with her exclamations. When she had passed the door about ten steps, Ned permitted me to cover my frozen foot with my boot, and we moved on towards the fire. We soon overtook the woman just mentioned, who had become somewhat pacified. As Ned came along side of her, without seeming to notice her, he observed "Poor Dalby, I see his house is gone."

"I said so," she screamed out—"I knew it!"—and on she went, screaming ten times louder than before.

As soon as we reached the fire, a gentleman in military dress rode up and ordered Ned into the line, to hand buckets. Ned stept in, and the first bucket that was handed to him, he raised it very deliberately to his mouth, and began to drink. In a few seconds, all on Ned's right, were overburdened with buckets, and calling loudly for relief, while those on his left were unemployed. Terrible was the cursing and clamor, and twenty voices at once ordered Ned out of the line. Ned stept out, and along came the man on horse back, and ordered him in again.

"Captain," said Ned, "I am so thirsty that I can do nothing until I can get some water, and they will not let me drink in the line."

"Well," said the Captain, "step in, and I'll see that you get a drink."

Ned stept in again, and receiving the first bucket, began to raise it to his lips very slowly, when some one halloed to him to pass on the bucket, and he brought it down again, and handed it on.

"Why did'nt you drink?" said the Captain.

"Why don't you see they won't let me?" said Ned.

"Don't mind what they say—drink, and then go on with your work."

Ned took the next bucket, and commenced raising it as before, when some one again ordered him to pass on the bucket.

"There," said Ned, turning to the Captain, with the bucket half-raised, "you hear that?"

"Why, blast your eyes," said the Captain, "what do you stop for? Drink on and have done with it."

Ned raised the bucket to his lips and drank, or pretended to drink, until a horse might have been satisfied.

"Ain't you done?" said the Captain, general mutiny and complaint beginning to prevail in the line.

"Why ha'nt you drank enough?" said the Captain becoming extremely impatient.

"Most," said Ned, letting out a long breath, and still holding the bucket near his lips.

"Zounds and blood!" cried the Captain, "clear yourself —you'll drink an engine full of water."

Ned left the ranks, and went to his lodgings; and the rising sun found us on our way homeward.

HALL.

THE FIGHT.

IN the younger days of the Republic, there lived in the county of ———, two men, who were admitted on all hands to be the very *best men* in the county—which, in the Georgia vocabulary, means they could flog any other two men in the county. Each, through many a hard fought battle, had acquired the mastery of his own battalion; but they lived on opposite sides of the Court House, and in different battalions: consequently they were but seldom thrown together. When they met, however, they were always very friendly; indeed, at their first interview, they seemed to conceive a wonderful attachment to each other, which rather increased than diminished, as they became better acquainted; so that, but for the circumstance which I am about to mention, the question which had been a thousand times asked "Which is the best man, Billy Stallions, (Stallings,) or Bob Durham?" would probably never have been answered.

Billy ruled the upper battalion, and Bob the lower. The former measured six feet and an inch, in his stockings, and without a single pound of cumbrous flesh about him weighed a hundred and eighty. The latter, was an inch shorter than his rival, and ten pounds lighter; but he was much the most active of the two. In running and jumping, he had but few equals in the county; and in wrestling, not one. In other respects they were nearly equal. Both were admirable specimens of human nature in its finest form. Billy's victories had generally been achieved by the tremendous power of his blows; one of which had often proved decisive of his battles;

Bob's, by his adroitness in bringing his adversary to the ground. This advantage he had never failed to gain, at the onset, and when gained, he never failed to improve it to the defeat of his adversary. These points of difference, have involved the reader in a doubt, as to the probable issue of a contest between them. It was not so, however, with the two battalions. Neither had the least difficulty in determining the point by the most natural and irresistible deductions *a priori:* and though, by the same course of reasoning, they arrived at directly opposite conclusions, neither felt its confidence in the least shaken by this circumstance. The upper battalion swore "that Billy only wanted one lick at him to knock his heart, liver and lights out of him; and if he got two at him, he'd knock him into a cocked hat." The lower battalion retorted, "that he would'nt have time to double his fist, before Bob would put his head where his feet ought to be; and that, by the time he hit the ground, the meat would fly off his face so quick, that people would think it was shook off by the fall." These disputes often lead to the *argumentum ad hominem;* but with such equality of success on both sides, as to leave the main question just where they found it. They usually ended, however, in the common way, with a bet; and many a quart of old Jamaica, (whiskey had not then supplanted rum,) were staked upon the issue. Still, greatly to the annoyance of the curious, Billy and Bob continued to be good friends.

Now there happened to reside in the county, just alluded to, a little fellow, by the name of Ransy Sniffle: a sprout of Richmond, who, in his earlier days, had fed copiously upon red clay and blackberries. This diet had given to Ransy a complexion that a corpse would have disdained to own, and an abdominal rotundity that was quite unprepossessing. Long spells of the fever and ague, too, in Ransy's youth, had conspired with clay and blackberries, to throw him quite out of the order of nature. His shoulders were fleshless and elevated; his head large and flat; his neck slim and translucent; and his arms, hands, fingers and feet, were lengthened out of all proportion to the rest of his frame. His joints were large, and his limbs small; and as for flesh, he could not with propriety be said to have any. Those parts which nature usually supplies with the most of this article—the calves of the legs for example—presented in him the appearance of so many well drawn blisters. His height was just five feet nothing; and his average weight in blackberry season, ninety-five. I have been thus particular in describing him, for the purpose of showing what a great matter a little fire sometimes kindleth. There was nothing on this earth which delighted Ransy so much as a fight. He never seemed fairly alive, except when he was witnessing, fomenting, or talking about a fight. Then, indeed, his deep sunken grey eye, assumed something of a living fire; and his tongue acquired a volubility that bordered upon eloquence. Ransy had been kept for more than a year in the most torturing suspense, as to the comparative manhood of Billy Stallings and Bob Durham. He had resorted to all his usual expedients to bring them in collision, and had entirely failed. He had faithfully reported to Bob all that had been said by the people in the upper battalion "agin him," and "he was sure Billy Stallings started it. He heard Bill say himself, to Jim Brown, that he could whip him, *or any other man in his battalion;*" and this he told to Bob—adding, "Dod durn his soul, if he was a little bigger, if he'd let any man *put upon* his battalion in such a way." Bob replied, "If he, (Stallings) thought so, he'd better come and try it." This Ransy carried to Billy, and delivered it with a spirit becoming his own dignity, and the character of his battalion, and with a coloring well calculated to give it effect. These, and many other schemes which Ransy laid, for the gratification of his curiosity, entirely failed of their object. Billy and Bob continued friends, and Ransy had begun to lapse into the most tantalizing and hopeless despair, when a circumstance occurred, which led to a settlement of the long disputed question.

Ransy Sniffle

It is said that a hundred game cocks will live in perfect harmony together, if you will not put a hen with them: and so it would have been with Billy and Bob, had there been no women in the world. But there were women in the world, and from them, each of our heroes had taken to himself a wife. The good ladies were no strangers to the prowess of their husbands, and strange as it may seem, they presumed a little upon it.

The two battalions had met at the Court House, upon a regimental parade. The two champions were there, and their wives had accompanied them. Neither knew the other's lady, nor were the ladies known to each other. The exercises of the day were just over, when Mrs. Stallings and Mrs. Durham stept simultaneously into the store of Zepheniah Atwater, from "down east."

"Have you any Turkey-red?" said Mrs. S.

"Have you any curtain calico?" said Mrs. D. at the same moment.

"Yes, ladies," said Mr. Atwater, "I have both."

"Then help me first," said Mrs. D., "for I'm in a hurry."

"I'm in as great a hurry as she is," said Mrs. S., "and I'll thank you to help me first."

"And pray, who are you, madam!" continued the other.

"Your betters, madam," was the reply.

At this moment Billy Stallings stept in. "Come," said he, "Nancy, let's be going; it's getting late."

"I'd o' been gone half an hour ago," she replied, "if it had'nt o' been for that impudent huzzy."

"Who do you call an impudent huzzy? you nasty, good-for-nothing, snaggle-toothed gaub of fat, you," returned Mrs. D.

"Look here woman," said Billy, "have you got a husband here? If you have, I'll *lick* him till he learns to teach you better manners, you *sassy* heifer you." At this moment something was seen to rush out of the store, as if ten thousand hornets were stinging it; crying "Take care—let me go —don't hold me—where's Bob Durham?" It was Ransy Sniffle, who had been listening in breathless delight, to all that had passed.

"Yonder's Bob, setting on the Court-house steps," cried one. "What's the matter?"

"Don't talk to me!" said Ransy. "Bob Durham, you'd better go long yonder, and take care of your wife. They're playing h—l with her there, in Zeph. Atwater's store. Dod deternally durn my soul, if any man was to talk to my wife as Bill Stallions is talking to yours, if I did'nt drive blue blazes through him in less than no time."

Bob sprang to the store in a minute, followed by a hundred friends; for the bully of a county never wants friends.

"Bill Stallions," said Bob, as he entered, "what have you been saying to my wife?"

"Is that your wife?" inquired Billy, obviously much surprised, and a little disconcerted.

"Yes, she is, and no man shall abuse her, I don't care who he is."

"Well," rejoined Billy, "it an't worth while to go over it —I've said enough for a fight: and if you'll step out, we'll settle it!"

"Billy," said Bob, "are you for a fair fight?"

"I am," said Billy. "I've heard much of your manhood, and I believe I'm a better man than you are. If you will go into a ring with me, we can soon settle the dispute."

"Choose your friends," said Bob; "make your ring, and I'll be in it with mine, as soon as you will."

They both stept out, and began to strip very deliberately; each battalion gathering round its champion—except Ransy, who kept himself busy, in a most honest endeavor to hear and see all that transpired in both groups, at the same time. He ran from one to the other, in quick succession— peeped here, and listened there—talked to this one—then to that one—and then to himself—squatted under one's legs, and another's arms; and in the short interval between stripping and stepping into the ring, managed to get himself trod on by half of both battalions. But Ransy was not the only one interested upon this occasion:—the most intense interest prevailed every where. Many were the conjectures, doubts, oaths and imprecations uttered, while the parties were preparing for the combat. All the knowing ones were consulted as to the issue; and they all agreed to a man, in one of two opinions: either that Bob would flog Billy, or Billy would flog Bob. We must be permitted, however, to dwell for a moment upon the opinion of 'Squire Thomas Loggins; a man, who it was said, had never failed to predict the issue of a fight, in all his life. Indeed, so unerring had he always proved, in this regard, that it would have been counted the most obstinate infidelity, to doubt for a moment, after he had delivered himself. 'Squire Loggins was a man who said but little; but that little was always delivered with the most imposing solemnity of look and cadence. He always wore the aspect of profound thought, and you could not look at him without coming to the conclusion, that he was elaborating truth from its most intricate combinations.

"Uncle Tommy," said Sam Reynolds, "you can tell us all about it, if you will—how will the fight go?"

The question immediately drew an anxious group around the 'Squire. He raised his teeth slowly from the head of his walking cane, on which they had been resting—pressed his lips closely and thoughtfully together—threw down his eye brows—dropped his chin—raised his eyes to an angle of twenty three degrees—paused about half a minute, and replied: "Sammy, watch Robert Durham close in the beginning of the fight—take care of William Stallions in the middle of it—and see who has the wind at the end." As he uttered the last member of the sentence, he looked slily at Bob's friends, and winked very significantly; whereupon they rushed, with one accord, to tell Bob what Uncle Tommy had said. As they retired, the 'Squire turned to Billy's friends, and said, with a smile: "Them boys think I mean that Bob will whip."

Here the other party kindled into joy, and hastened to inform Billy how Bob's friends had deceived themselves as to Uncle Tommy's opinion. In the meantime, the principals and seconds, were busily employed in preparing themselves for the combat. The plan of attack and defence, the manner of improving the various turns of the conflict, "the best mode of saving wind," &c. &c. were all discussed and settled. At length, Billy announced himself ready, and his crowd were seen moving to the centre of the Court House Square; he and his five seconds in the rear. At the same time, Bob's party moved to the same point, and in the same order. The ring was now formed, and for a moment the silence of death reigned through both battalions. It was soon interrupted, however, by the cry of "clear the way!" from Billy's seconds; when the ring opened in the centre of the upper battalion, (for the order of march had arranged the centre of the two battalions on opposite sides of the circle,) and Billy stept into the ring from the east, followed by his friends. He was stript to the trowsers, and exhibited an arm, breast and shoulders, of the most tremendous portent. His step was firm, daring and martial; and as he bore his fine form a little in advance of his friends, an involuntary burst of triumph broke from his side of the ring; and at the same moment, an uncontrollable thrill of awe, ran along the whole curve of the lower battalion.

"Look at him!" was heard from his friends—"just look at him."

"Ben, how much you ask to stand before that man two seconds?"

"Pshaw, don't talk about it! Just thinkin' about it's broke three o' my ribs a'ready!"

"What's Bob Durham going to do, when Billy lets that arm loose upon him?"

"God bless your soul, he'll think thunder and lightning a mint julip to it."

"Oh, look here men, go take Bill Stallions out o' that ring, and bring in Phil Johnson's stud horse, so that Durham may have some chance! I don't want to see the man killed right away."

These and many other like expressions, interspersed thickly with oaths of the most modern coinage, were coming from all points of the upper battalion, while Bob was adjusting the girth of his pantaloons, which walking had discovered, not to be exactly right. It was just fixed to his mind, his foes becoming a little noisy, and his friends a little uneasy at his delay, when Billy called out, with a smile of some meaning, "Where's the bully of the lower battalion? I'm getting tired of waiting."

"Here he is," said Bob, lighting, as it seemed from the clouds in the ring, for he had actually bounded clear of the head of Ransy Sniffle, into the circle. His descent was quite as imposing as Billy's entry, and excited the same feelings, but in opposite bosoms.

Voices of exultation now rose on his side.

"Where did he come from?"

"Why," said one of his seconds, (all having just entered,) "we were girting him up, about a hundred yards out yonder, when he heard Billy ask for the bully; and he fetched a leap over the Court House, and went out of sight; but I told them to come on, they'd find him here."

Here the lower battalion burst into a peal of laughter, mingled with a look of admiration, which seemed to denote their entire belief of what they had heard.

"Boys widen the ring, so as to give him room to jump."

"Oh, my little flying wild cat, hold him if you can! and when you get him fast, hold lightning next."

"Ned what you think he's made of?"

"Steel-springs and chicken-hawk, God bless you!"

"Gentlemen," said one of Bob's seconds, "I understand it is to be a fair fight; catch as catch can, rough and tumble:— no man touch 'till one or the other hollos."

"That's the rule," was the reply from the other side.

"Are you ready?"

"We are ready."

"Then blaze away my game cocks!"

At the word, Bob dashed at his antagonist at full speed; and Bill squared himself to receive him with one of his most fatal blows. Making his calculation from Bob's velocity, of the time when he would come within striking distance, he let drive with tremendous force. But Bob's onset was obviously planned to avoid this blow; for contrary to all expectations, he stopt short just out of arms reach; and before Billy could recover his balance—Bob had him "all underhold." The next second, sure enough, "found Billy's head where his feet ought to be." How it was done, no one could tell; but as if by supernatural power, both Billy's feet were thrown full half his own height in the air, and he came down with a force that seemed to shake the earth. As he struck the ground, commingled shouts, screams and yells burst from the lower battalion, loud enough to be heard for miles. "Hurra my little hornet!"—"Save him!"—"Feed him!—Give him the Durham physic till his stomach turns!" Billy was no sooner down than Bob was on him, and lending him awful blows about the face and breast. Billy made two efforts to rise by main strength, but failed. "Lord bless you man, don't try to get up!—*Lay* still and take it!—you *bleege* to have it."

Billy now turned his face suddenly to the ground, and rose upon his hands and knees. Bob jirked up both his hands and threw him on his face. He again recovered his late position, of which Bob endeavored to deprive him as before; but missing one arm, he failed, and Billy rose. But he had scarcely resumed his feet before they flew up as before, and he came again to the ground. "No fight gentlemen!" cried Bob's friends, "the man can't stand up!—Bouncing feet are bad things to fight in." His fall, however, was this time comparatively light; for having thrown his right arm round Bob's neck, he carried his head down with him. This grasp, which was obstinately maintained, prevented Bob from getting on him, and they lay head to head, seeming, for a time, to do nothing. Presently they rose, as if by mutual consent; and as they rose, a shout broke from both battalions. "Oh, my lark!" cried the east, "has he foxed you? Do you begin to feel him! He's only beginning to fight—He ain't got warm yet."

"Look yonder!" cried the west—"did'nt I tell you so! He

hit the ground so hard, it jarred his nose off. Now ain't he a pretty man as he stands? He shall have my sister Sall just for his pretty looks. I want to get in the breed of them sort o' men, to drive ugly out of my kin folks."

I looked and saw that Bob had entirely lost his left ear, and a large piece from his left cheek. His right eye was a little discolored, and the blood flowed profusely from his wounds.

Bill presented a hideous spectacle. About a third of his nose, at the lower extremity, was bit off, and his face so swelled and bruised, that it was difficult to discover in it any thing of the human visage—much more the fine features which he carried into the ring.

They were up only long enough for me to make the foregoing discoveries, when down they went again, precisely as before. They no sooner touched the ground than Bill relinquished his hold upon Bob's neck. In this, he seemed to all, to have forfeited the only advantage which put him upon an equality with his adversary. But the movement was soon explained. Bill wanted this arm for other purposes than defence; and he had made arrangements whereby he knew that he could make it answer these purposes; for when they rose again, he had the middle finger of Bob's left hand in his mouth. He was now secure from Bob's annoying trips; and he began to lend his adversary most tremendous blows, every one of which was hailed by a shout from his friends. "Bullets!—*Hoss* kicking!—Thunder!"—"That'll do for the face—now feel his short ribs, Billy!"

I now considered the contest settled. I deemed it impossible for any human being to withstand for five seconds, the loss of blood which issued from Bob's ear, check, nose and

finger, accompanied with such blows as he was receiving.
Still he maintained the conflict, and gave blow for blow
with considerable effect. But the blows of each became
slower and weaker, after the first three or four; and it became obvious, that Bill wanted the room, which Bob's finger occupied, for breathing. He would therefore, probably,
in a short time, have let it go, had not Bob anticipated his
politeness, by jirking away his hand, and making him a
present of the finger. He now seized Bill again, and brought
him to his knees—but he recovered. He again brought him
to his knees; and he again recovered. A third effort, however, brought him down, and Bob on top of him. These efforts seemed to exhaust the little remaining strength of both;
and they lay, Bill undermost, and Bob across his breast,
motionless, and panting for breath. After a short pause, Bob
gathered his hand full of dirt and sand, and was in the act
of grinding it in his adversary's eyes, when Bill cried
"ENOUGH!"—Language cannot describe the scene which
followed—the shouts, oaths, frantic jestures, taunts, replies
and little fights; and therefore I shall not attempt it. The
champions were borne off by their seconds, and washed:
when many a bleeding wound, and ugly bruise, was discovered on each, which no eye had seen before.

Many had gathered round Bob, and were in various ways
congratulating and applauding him, when a voice from the
centre of the circle cried out: "Boys, hush and listen to me!"
It proceeded from Squire Loggins, who had made his way
to Bob's side, and had gathered his face up into one of its
most flattering and intelligible expressions. All were obedient to the Squire's command. "Gentlemen," continued he,
with a most knowing smile, "is—Sammy—Reynold—in—

this—company—of—gentlemen." "Yes," said Sam, "here I am." "Sammy," said the Squire, winking to the company, and drawing the head of his cane to his mouth with an arch smile, as he closed, "I—wish—you—to tell—cousin—Bob-by—and—these—gentlemen here present—what—your—uncle — Tommy — said — before — the — fight — began?" "Oh! get away, uncle Tom," says Sam, smiling, (the Squire winked,) "you don't know nothing about *fighting*." (The 'Squire winked again.) "All you know about it, is how it'll begin; how it'll go on; how it'll end; that's all. Cousin Bob, when you going to fight again, just go to the old man, and let him tell you all about it. If he can't, don't ask no-body else nothing about it, I tell you." The Squire's fore-sight was complimented in many ways by the by-standers; and he retired, advising "the boys to be at peace, as fighting was a bad business."

Durham and Stallings kept their beds for several weeks, and did not meet again for two months. When they met, Billy stepped up to Bob and offered his hand, saying: "Bob-by you've *licked* me a fair fight; but you would'nt have done it, if I had'nt been in the wrong. I ought'nt to have treated your wife as I did; and I felt so through the whole fight; and it sort o' cowed me."

"Well Billy," said Bob, "let's be friends. Once in the fight, when you had my finger in your mouth, and was pealing me in the face and breast, I was going to hollo; but I thought of Betsy, and knew the house would be too hot for me, if I got whipt, when fighting for her, after always whip-ping when I fought for myself."

"Now, that's what I always love to see," said a bystand-er: "It's true, I brought about the fight; but I would'nt have done it, if it had'nt o' been on account of *Miss*, (Mrs.) Durham. But dod deternally durn my soul, if I ever could stand by and see any woman put upon—much less *Miss* Durham. If Bobby had'nt been there, I'd o' took it up myself, be durned if I would'nt, even if I'd o' got whipt for it— But we're all friends now." The reader need hardly be told, this was Ransy Sniffle.

Thanks to the Christian religion, to schools, colleges, and benevolent associations, such scenes of barbarism and cruelty, as that which I have been just describing, are now of rare occurrence: though they may still be occasionally met with in some of the new counties. Wherever they prevail, they are a disgrace to that community. The peace officers who countenance them, deserve a place in the Penitentiary.

HALL.

THE SONG.

IT is not to avoid the malediction of Shakspeare, upon such "as have not music in themselves—and are not charmed with the concord of sweet sounds," that I profess to be fond of music; but because I am, in truth, extravagantly fond of it. But I am not fond of French music; and as for the Italian, I think that any one who will dare to inflict it upon an American ear, ought to be sent to the Penitentiary, without a trial. It is true that some of the simple,

national French airs, are very fine; but there is not one in
one thousand Italian tunes, simple or compound, which is
not *manslaughter*. The German compositions are decidedly
the best from the continent of Europe; but even these are, of
late, partaking so much of the vices of France and Italy,
that they have become scarcely sufferable. As yet, however,
they may be safely admitted into a land of liberty and sense.
Scotland has escaped the corruptions which have crept into
the empire of music, and consequently her music recom-
mends itself, with irresistible charms, to every ear which is
not vitiated by the senseless rattle of the continent. Ireland
is a little more contaminated; but still her compositions re-
tain enough of their primitive simplicity and sweetness, to
entitle them to the patronage of all who would cultivate a
correct taste in this interesting department of the fine arts.
I would not be understood as speaking here without any
limitations or restrictions; but I do maintain, that with
some few exceptions, all of the soul of music, which is now
left in the world, is to be found in Scotland or Ireland.

But Germans, Frenchmen and Italians, are decidedly the
best,—that is, *the most expert* performers in the world. They
perform all over the world, and in order to exhibit themselves to the best advantage, they select the most difficult
and complicated pieces. The people at large, presume that
the best performers must be the best judges of music, and
must make the best selections; they therefore forego the
trouble of forming an opinion of their own, and pin their
faith upon the decisions—or rather the practice, of the ama-
teurs. It was somehow in this way, I presume, that the
fashionable music of the day, first obtained currency. Having become prevalent, it has become tolerable; just as has

the use of tobacco or ardent spirits. And while upon this head, I would earnestly recommend to the friends of reform in our favored country, to establish an "Anti-mad-music Society," in order to suppress, if possible, the cruelties of our modern musical *entertainments*.

If the instrumental music of France and Italy be bad, their vocal music is, if possible, a thousand times worse. Neither the English, *nor the Georgia language*, furnishes me with a term expressive of the horrors of a French or Italian song, as it is agonized forth by one of their professed singers. The law should make it justifiable homicide in any man, to kill an Italian in the very act of inflicting an *il penseroso* upon a refined American ear.

And yet with all the other European abominations which have crept into our highly favoured country, the French and Italian style of singing and playing, has made its way hither; and it is not uncommon to hear our boarding-school Misses piping away, not merely in the style, but in the very language of these nations.—This I can bear very well, if there happen to be a Frenchman or Italian present, because I know that he suffers more from the *words*, than I do from the *music*; for I confess, that upon such occasions, I feel something of the savage malignity, which visits the sins of a nation upon any of its citizens. But it most frequently happens that I am put to the tortures of which I have been speaking, without this mitigation. It was thus with me a few evenings ago, at Mrs. B——'s party.

Tea had been disposed of, and the nonsensical chit-chat of such occasions had begun to flag, when I invited Miss Mary Williams to the piano. She rose promptly at my request, without any affected airs, and with no other apology, than that "she felt some diffidence at playing in the presence of *Miss Crump*." The piano was an admirable one; and its tones were exquisitely fine. Mary seated herself at it, and after a short, but beautiful prelude, she commenced one of Burns' plaintive songs, to a tune which was new to me, but which was obviously from the poet's own land, and by one who felt the inspiration of his verse. The composer and the poet were both honored by the performer. Mary's voice was inimitably fine. Her enunciation was clear and distinct, with just emphasis enough to give the verse its appropriate expression, without interrupting the melody of the music; and her modulations were perfect.

She had closed, and was in the act of rising, before I awoke from the delightful reverie into which she had lulled me. I arrested her, however, and insisted upon her proceeding; when she gave me one of Allan Ramsey's best, to measure equally appropriate. This she followed with Tannahill's "Gloomy Winter's Noo Awa," and was again retiring, when my friend Hall observed—"See Miss Mary, you've brought a tear to Mr. Baldwin's eye, and you must not cease until you chase it away with some lively air." My friend was right—The touching pathos of Mary's voice, conspiring with a train of reflections, which the song inspired, had really brought me to tears. I thought of poor Tannahill's fate. He was the victim of a Book-seller's stupidity. With men of taste and letters, his fugitive pieces, particularly his lyrics, had gained him a well-deserved reputation; but he was not exempt from the common lot of authors. He was attacked by the ignorant and the invidious; and with the hopeless design of silencing these, he prepared a volume or more of his poems, with great care, and sent them to a

Book-seller for publication. After the lapse of several weeks, they were returned without a compliment, or an offer for them. The mortification and disappointment were too severe for his reason. It deserted him, and soon after, he was found dead in a tunnel of the burn, which had been the scene of one of his earliest songs. Unfortunately, in his madness, he destroyed his favorite works.

Such was the train of reflection, from which Mary was kind enough, at the request of my friend, to relieve me, by a lively Irish air. Had it not been admirably selected, I could hardly have borne the transition. But there was enough of softening melody, mingled with the sprightliness of the air, to lead me gently to a gayer mood;—in which she left me.

In the meantime, most of the young ladies and gentlemen had formed a circle round Miss Aurelia Emma Theodosia Augusta Crump, and were earnestly engaged in pressing her to play. One young lady even went so far as to drop on her knees before her, and in this posture to beseech "her dear Augusta, just to play the delightful overture of ——
—," something that sounded to me like "*Blaze in the frets.*" This petition was urged with such a melting sweetness of voice, such a bewitching leer at the gentlemen, and such a theatric heave of the bosom, that it threw the young gentlemen into transports. Hall was rude enough to whisper in mine ear, "that he thought it indelicate to expose an unmantled bosom to a perpendicular view of a large company;" and he muttered something about "republican simplicity," I knew not exactly what. But I assured him, the fair petitioner was so overcome by her solicitude for the overture, that she thought of nothing else, and was wholly unconscious that there was a gentleman in the room. As to his insinuation about "points of view," I convinced him by

an easy argument that it was wholly unfounded; for that this was the very point of view in which an exposed neck must always be seen, while men continue taller than women; and that, as the young lady must have been apprised of this, she would hardly take so much trouble for nothing. But to return.

Miss Crump was inexorable—She declared that she was entirely out of practice. "She scarcely ever touched the piano"—"Mamma was always scolding her for giving so much of her time to French and Italian, and neglecting her music and painting; but she told mamma the other day, that it really was so irksome to her to quit Racine and Dante, and go to thrumming upon the piano, that but for the obligations of filial obedience, she did not think she should ever touch it again."

Here Mrs. Crump was kind enough by the merest accident in the world, to interpose, and to relieve the company from further anxiety.

"Augusta, my dear," said she, "go and play a tune or two; the company will excuse your hoarseness."

Miss Crump rose immediately, at her mother's bidding, and moved to the piano, accompanied by a large group of smiling faces.

"Poor child," said Mrs. Crump as she went forward, "she is frightened to death. I wish Augusta could overcome her diffidence."

Miss Crump was educated at Philadelphia; she had been taught to sing by Madam Piggisqueaki, who was a pupil of Ma'm'selle Crokifroggietta, who had sung with Madam Catalani; and she had taken lessons on the piano, from Seignor Buzzifussi, who had played with Paganini.

She seated herself at the piano, rocked to the right, then

to the left—leaned forward, then backward, and began. She placed her right hand about midway the keys, and her left about two octaves below it. She now put off the right in a brisk canter up the treble notes, and the left after it. The left then led the way back, and the right pursued it in like manner. The right turned, and repeated its first movement; but the left outran it this time, hopt over it, and flung it entirely off the track. It came in again, however, behind the left on its return, and passed it in the same style. They now became highly incensed at each other, and met furiously on the middle ground. Here a most awful conflict ensued, for about the space of ten seconds, when the right whipped off all of a sudden, as I thought, fairly vanquished. But I was in the error against which Jack Randolph cautions us—"It had only fallen back to a stronger position." It mounted upon two black keys, and commenced the note of a rattlesnake. This had a wonderful effect upon the left, and placed the doctrine of "snake charming" beyond dispute. The left rushed furiously towards it repeatedly, but seemed invariably panic-struck, when it came within six keys of it; and as invariably retired with a tremendous roaring down the bass keys. It continued its assaults, sometimes by the way of the naturals, sometimes by the way of the sharps, and sometimes by a zigzag, through both; but all its attempts to dislodge the right from its strong hold, proving ineffectual, it came close up to its adversary, and expired.

Any one, or rather no one, can imagine what kind of noises the piano gave forth, during the conflict. Certain it is, no one can describe them, and therefore I shall not attempt it.

The battle ended—Miss Augusta moved as though she

would have arisen, but this was protested against by a number of voices at once: "One song, my dear Aurelia," said
Miss Small; "you must sing that sweet little French air you
used to sing in Philadelphia, and which Madam Piggisqueaki was so fond of."

Miss Augusta looked pitifully at her mama; and her mama looked "sing" at Miss Augusta: accordingly she squared
herself for a song.

She brought her hands to the campus this time in fine
style, and they seemed now to be perfectly reconciled to
each other. They commenced a kind of colloquy; the right
whispering treble very softly, and the left responding bass
very loudly. The conference had been kept up until I began
to desire a change of the subject, when my ear caught, indistinctly, some very curious sounds, which appeared to
proceed from the lips of Miss Augusta—they seemed to be
compounded of a dry cough, a grunt, a hiccup and a whisper; and they were introduced, it appeared to me, as inter-
preters between the right and left. Things progressed in this
way for about the space of fifteen seconds, when I happened
to direct my attention to Mr. Jenkins, from Philadelphia.
His eyes were closed, his head rolled gracefully from side to
side; a beam of heavenly complacency rested upon his
countenance; and his whole man gave irresistible demon-
stration that Miss Crump's music made him feel good all
over. I had just turned from the contemplation of Mr. Jenkins' transports, to see whether I could extract from the performance any thing intelligible, when Miss Crump made a
fly-catching grab at a half dozen keys in a row, and at the
same instant she fetched a long dunghill-cock crow, at the
conclusion of which she grabbed as many keys with the left.

This came over Jenkins like a warm bath; and over me, like a rake of bamboo briers.

My nerves had not recovered from this shock, before Miss Augusta repeated the movement, and accompanied it with the squall of a pinched cat. This threw me into an ague fit, but from respect to the performer, I maintained my position. She now made a third grasp with the right, boxed the faces of six keys in a row with the left, and at the same time raised one of the most unearthly howls that ever issued from the throat of a human being. This seemed the signal for universal uproar and destruction. She now threw away all reserve, and charged the piano with her whole force.—She boxed it, she clawed it, she raked it, she scraped it. Her neckvein swelled, her chin flew up, her face flushed, her eye glared, her bosom heaved—She screamed, she howled, she yelled, cackled, and was in the act of dwelling upon the note of a screech owl, when I took the St. Vitus' dance, and rushed out of the room. "Good Lord," said a by-stander, "if this be her *singing*, what must her *crying be!*" As I reached the door, I heard a voice exclaim, "By heavens! she's the most enchanting performer I ever heard in my life!" I turned to see who was the author of this ill-timed compliment; and who should it be but Nick Truck, from Lincoln, who seven years before, was dancing "Possum up the Gum Tree," in the chimney corner of his father's kitchen. Nick had entered the counting-room of a merchant in Charleston some five or six years before; had been sent out as super-cargo of a vessel to Bordeaux, and while the vessel was de-livering one cargo, and taking in another, had contracted a wonderful relish for French music.

As for myself, I went home in convulsions, took sixty drops of laudanum, and fell asleep. I dreamt that I was in a beautiful city, the streets of which intersected each other at right angles—That the birds of the air, and the beasts of the forest had gathered there for battle; the former, led on by a Frenchman, the latter by an Italian—That I was looking on their movements towards each other, when I heard the cry of "Hecate is coming!" I turned my eye to the north east, and saw a female flying through the air towards the city, and distinctly recognized in her, the features of Miss Crump. I took the alarm, and was making my escape, when she gave command for the beasts and birds to fall on me.— They did so, and with all the noises of the animal world, were in the act of tearing me to pieces, when I was waked by the stepping of Hall, my room-mate into bed.

"Oh, my dear sir," exclaimed I, "you have waked me from a horrible dream. What o'clock is it?"

"Ten minutes after twelve," said he.

"And where have you been to this late hour?"

"I have just returned from the party."

"And what kept you so late?"

"Why, I disliked to retire while Miss Crump was playing."

"In mercy's name!" said I, "is she playing yet?"

"Yes," said he, "I had to leave her playing at last."

"And where was Jenkins?"

"He was there, still in ecstasies, and urging her to play on."

"And where was Truck?"

"He was asleep."

"And what was she playing?"

"An Italian ———."

Here I swooned, and heard no more.

                                        BALDWIN.

THE TURN OUT.

IN the good old days of *fescues*, *abisselfas*, and *anpersants*,* terms which used to be familiar in this country during the Revolutionary war, and which lingered in some of our county schools for a few years afterwards, I visited my friend, Captain Griffin, who resided about seven miles to the eastward of Wrightsborough, then in Richmond, but now in Columbia county. I reached the Captain's hospitable home on Easter, and was received by him and his good lady, with a *Georgia welcome* of 1790. It was warm from the heart, and taught me in a moment, that all the obligations of the visit were upon their side, not mine. Such receptions were not peculiar, at that time, to the Captain and his family; they were common throughout the State. Where are they now! and where the generous hospitalities which invariably followed them! I see them occasionally at the contented farmer's door, and at his festive board, but when they shall have taken leave of these, Georgia will know them no more.

The day was consumed in the interchange of news between the Captain and myself, (though I confess it might have been better employed,) and the night found us seated round a temporary fire, which the Captain's sons had kin-

* The *fescue* was a sharpened wire, or other instrument, used by the preceptor, to point out the letters to the children.

Abisselfa is a contraction of the words "a, by itself, a." It was usual, when either of the vowels constituted a syllable of a word, to pronounce it and denote its independent character, by the words just mentioned, thus: "a by itself, *a*-c-o-r-n corn, *acorn*."—"e by itself, *e*-v-i-l, *evil*, &c."

The character which stands for the word "*and*" (&) was probably pronounced by the same accompaniment, but in terms borrowed from the Latin language, thus: "& *per se* (by itself) &." Hence, "anpersant."

dled up for the purpose of dying eggs. It was a common custom of those days with boys, to dye and peck eggs on Easter Sunday, and for a few days afterwards. They were colored according to the fancy of the dyer; some yellow, some green, some purple, and some with a variety of colors, borrowed from a piece of calico. They were not unfrequently beautified with a taste and skill which would have extorted a compliment from Hezekiah Niles, if he had seen them a year ago, in the hands of the *"young operatives,"* in some of the northern manufactories. No sooner was the work of dying finished, than our "young operatives" sallied forth to stake the whole proceeds of their *"domestic industry"* upon a peck. Egg was struck against egg, point to point, and the egg which was broken was given up as lost to the owner of the one which came whole from the shock.

While the boys were busily employed in the manner just mentioned, the Captain's youngest son, George, gave us an anecdote highly descriptive of the Yankee and Georgia character, even in their buddings, and at this early date. "What you think, pa," said he, "Zeph. Pettibone went and got his Uncle Zach. to turn him a wooden egg; and he won a whole hat full o' eggs from all us boys 'fore we found it out —but when we found it out, may be John Brown did'nt smoke him for it, and took away all his eggs, and give 'em back to us boys;—and you think he did'nt go then and git a guinea-egg, and win most as many more, and John Brown would o' give it to him agin, if all we boys had'nt said we thought it was fair. I never see such a boy as that Zeph. Pettibone, in all my life. He don't mind whipping no more 'an nothing at all, if he can win eggs."

This anecdote, however, only fell in by accident, for

there was an all-absorbing subject which occupied the minds of the boys, during the whole evening, of which I could occasionally catch distant hints, in under tones and whispers, but of which I could make nothing, until they were afterwards explained by the Captain himself. Such as "I'll be bound Peet Jones and Bill Smith stretches him"— "By Jockey, soon as they seize him, you'll see me down upon him like a duck upon a Junebug." "By the time he touches the ground, he'll think he's got into a hornet's nest," &c.

"The boys," said the Captain, as they retired, "are going to turn out the school-master to-morrow, and you can perceive they think of nothing else. We must go over to the school-house, and witness the contest, in order to prevent injury to preceptor or pupils; for though the master is always upon such occasions, glad to be turned out, and only struggles long enough to present his patrons a fair apology for giving the children a holiday, which he desires as much as they do, the boys always conceive a holiday gained by a "turn out," as a sole achievement of their valor, and in their zeal to distinguish themselves, upon such memorable occasions, they sometimes become too rough, provoke the master to wrath, and a very serious conflict ensues. To prevent these consequences, to bear witness that the master was *forced* to yield, before he would withhold a day of his promised labor from his employers, and to act as a mediator between him and the boys, in settling the articles of peace, I always attend; and you must accompany me to-morrow." I cheerfully promised to do so.

The Captain and I rose before the sun, but the boys had risen, and were off to the school-house, before the dawn. After an early breakfast, hurried by Mrs. G. for our accommodation, my host and myself took up our line of march towards the school-house. We reached it about a half hour before the master arrived, but not before the boys had completed its fortifications. It was a simple log pen, about twenty feet square, with a door-way cut out of the logs, to which was fitted a rude door, made of clapboards, and swung on wooden hinges. The roof was covered with clapboards also, and retained in their places by heavy logs placed on them. The chimney was built of logs, diminishing in size from the ground to the top, and overspread inside and out with red clay mortar. The classic hut occupied a lovely spot, overshadowed by majestic hickorys, towering poplars, and strong armed oaks. The little plain on which it stood, was terminated at the distance of about fifty paces from its door, by the brow of a hill, which descended rather abruptly to a noble spring, that gushed joyously forth from among the roots of a stately beech, at its foot. The stream from this fountain scarcely burst in view, before it hid itself beneath the dark shade of a field of cane, which overspread the dale, through which it flowed, and marked its windings, until it turned from the sight, among vine-covered hills, at a distance far beyond that to which the eye could have traced it, without the help of its evergreen belt. A remark of the Captain's, as we viewed the lovely country around us, will give the reader my apology for the minuteness of the foregoing description. "These lands," said he, "will never wear out. Where they lie level, they will be as good fifty years hence as they are now." Forty-two years afterwards I visited the spot on which he stood, when he made the remark. The sun poured his whole strength upon the bald hill which once supported the sequestered school-house—Many a deep-washed gully met at a sickly bog, where gushed the limpid fountain—a dying willow rose from the soil which nourished the venerable beech—flocks wandered among the dwarf pines, and cropt a scanty meal from the vale, where the rich cane bowed and rustled to every breeze—and all around was barren, dreary and cheerless. But to return.

As I before remarked, the boys had strongly fortified the school-house, of which they had taken possession. The door was barricaded with logs, which I should have supposed would have defied the combined powers of the whole school. The chimney, too, was nearly filled with logs of goodly size; and these were the only passways to the interior. I concluded, if a *turn out* was all that was necessary to decide the contest in favor of the boys, they had already gained the victory. They had, however, not as much confidence in their outworks as I had, and therefore had armed themselves with long sticks; not for the purpose of using them upon the master, if the battle should come to close quarters, for this was considered unlawful warfare; but for the purpose of guarding their *works* from his approaches, which it was considered perfectly lawful to protect, by all manner of jobs and punches through the cracks. From the early assembling of the girls, it was very obvious that they had been let into the conspiracy, though they took no part in the active operations. They would, however, occasionally, drop a word of encouragement to the boys, such as "I would'nt turn out the master; but if I did turn him out, I'd die before I'd give up." These remarks doubtless had an emboldening effect upon "*the young freeborns*," as Mrs. Trollope would call them; for I never knew the Georgian of any age, who was indifferent to the smiles and praises of the ladies—before his marriage.

At length, Mr. Michael St. John, the school-master, made his appearance.—Though some of the girls had met him a quarter of a mile from the school-house, and told him all that had happened; he gave signs of sudden astonishment and indignation, when he advanced to the door, and was assailed by a whole platoon of sticks from the cracks: "Why, what does all this mean?" said he, as he approached the Captain and myself, with a countenance of two or three varying expressions.

"Why," said the Captain, "the boys have turned you out, because you have refused to give them an Easter holiday."

"Oh," returned Michael, "that's it, is it? Well, I'll see whether their parents are to pay me for letting their children play when they please." So saying, he advanced to the school-house, and demanded, in a lofty tone, of its inmates, an unconditional surrender.

"Well, give us holiday then," said twenty little urchins within, "and we'll let you in."

"Open the door of the *Academy*," (Michael would allow no body to call it a school-house)—"Open the door of the Academy this instant," said Michael, "or I'll break it down."

"Break it down," said Peet Jones and Bill Smith, "and we'll break you down."

During this colloquy I took a peep into the fortress, to see how the garrison were affected by the parley. The little ones were obviously panic struck at the first words of command; but their fears were all chased away by the bold determined reply of Peet Jones and Bill Smith, and they raised a whoop of defiance.

Michael now walked round the Academy three times, examining all its weak points with great care. He then paused, reflected for a moment, and wheeled off suddenly towards the woods, as though a bright thought had just struck him. He passed twenty things which I supposed he might be in quest of, such as huge stones, fence-rails, portable logs, and the like, without bestowing the least attention upon them. He went to one old log, searched it thoroughly, then to another, then to a hollow stump, peeped into it with great care, then to a hollow log, into which he looked with equal caution, and so on.

"What is he after?" enquired I.

"I'm sure I don't know," said the Captain, "but the boys do. Don't you notice the breathless silence which prevails in the school-house, and the intense anxiety with which they are eying him through the cracks?"

At this moment Michael had reached a little excavation at the root of a dog-wood, and was in the act of putting his hand into it, when a voice from the garrison exclaimed, with most touching pathos, "Lo'd o' messy, he's found my eggs! boys let's give up."

"I won't give up," was the reply from many voices at once.

"Rot your cowardly skin, Zeph. Pettibone, you would'nt give a wooden egg for all the holidays in the world."

If these replies did not reconcile Zepheniah to his apprehended loss, it at least silenced his complaints. In the meantime, Michael was employed in relieving Zeph's storehouse of its provisions; and truly its contents told well for Zeph's skill in egg-pecking. However, Michael took out the eggs with great care, and brought them within a few paces of the school-house, and laid them down with equal care, in full view of the besieged. He revisited the places which he had searched, and to which he seemed to have been led by intuition; for from nearly all of them did he draw eggs, in greater or less numbers. These he treated as he had done Zeph's; keeping each pile separate. Having arranged the eggs in double files before the door, he marched between them with an air of triumph, and once more demanded a surrender, under pain of an entire destruction of the garrison's provisions.

"Break 'em just as quick as you please," said George Griffin, "our mothers 'll give us a plenty more, won't they Pa?"

"I can answer for your's, my son," said the Captain; "she would rather give up every egg on the farm, than see you play the coward or traitor, to save your property."

Michael, finding that he could make no impression upon the fears or the avarice of the boys, determined to carry

Michael St. John, the School-Master, Effecting an Entrance by Storm

their fortifications by storm. Accordingly, he procured a heavy fence-rail, and commenced the assault upon the door. It soon came to pieces, and the upper logs fell out, leaving a space of about three feet at the top. Michael boldly entered the breach when by the articles of war, sticks were thrown aside, as no longer lawful weapons. He was resolutely met on the half demolished rampart by Peter Jones and William Smith, supported by James Griffin. These were the three largest boys in the school; the first about sixteen years of age, the second about fifteen, and the third just eleven. Twice was Michael repulsed by these young champions, but the third effort carried him fairly into the fortress. Hostilities now ceased for a while, and the Captain and I having levelled the remaining logs at the door, followed Michael into the house. A large three inch plank, (if it deserve that name, for it was wrought from the half of a tree's trunk, entirely with the axe,) attached to the logs by means of wooden pins, served the whole school for a writing desk. At a convenient distance below it, and on a line with it, stretched a smooth log, resting upon the logs of the house, which answered for the writers' seat. Michael took his seat upon the desk, placed his feet on the seat, and was sitting very composedly, when with a simultaneous movement, Peet and Bill seized each a leg, and marched off with it in quick time. The consequence is obvious—Michael's head first took the desk, then the seat, and finally the ground, (for the house was not floored,) with three sonorous thumps, of most doleful portent. No sooner did he touch the ground, than he was completely buried in boys. The three elder, laid themselves across his head, neck and breast, the rest arranging themselves *ad libitum*. Michael's equanimity was considerably disturbed by the first thump—became restive with the second, and took flight with the third. His first effort was to disengage his legs, for without them he could not rise, and to lie in his present position, was extremely inconvenient and undignified. Accordingly, he drew up his right, and kicked at random. This movement laid out about six in various directions upon the floor. Two rose crying—"Ding his old red-headed skin," said one of them, "to go and kick me right in my sore belly, where I fell down and raked it, running after that fellow that cried 'school-butter.' "*

"Drot his old snaggle-tooth picture," said the other, "to go and hurt my sore toe, where I knocked the nail off, going to the spring, to fetch a gourd of *warter* for him, and not for myself n'other."

"Hut!" said Capt. Griffin, "young Washingtons mind these trifles! At him again."

The name of Washington cured their wounds, and dried up their tears in an instant, and they legged him *de novo*. The left leg treated six more as unceremoniously as the right had those just mentioned—but the talismanic name, had just fallen upon their ears before the kick, so they were invulnerable. They therefore returned to the attack without loss of time. The struggle seemed to wax hotter and hotter,

---

* I have never been able to satisfy myself clearly, as to the literal meaning of these terms. They were considered an unpardonable insult to a country school, and always justified an attack by the whole fraternity, upon the person who used them in their hearing. I have known the scholars pursue a traveller two miles to be revenged of the insult. Probably they are a corruption of "The School's better."

"*Better*," was the term commonly used of old, to denote a *superior*, as it sometimes is in our day—"Wait till your *betters* are served," for example. I conjecture therefore, the expression just alluded to, was one of challenge, contempt and defiance, by which the person who used it, avowed himself the *superior* in all respects, of the whole school, from the preceptor down. If any one can give a better account of it, I shall be pleased to receive it.

for a short time after Michael came to the ground, and he threw the children about in all directions and postures, giving some of them thumps which would have placed the *ruffle-shirted* little darlings of the present day, under the discipline of paregoric and opodeldoc for a week; but these hardy sons of the forest, seemed not to feel them. As Michael's head grew easy, his limbs, by a natural sympathy became more quiet, and he now sued for peace, offering one day's holiday as the price. The boys demanded a week; but here the Captain interposed, and after the common, but often unjust custom of arbitrators, split the difference. In this instance the terms were equitable enough, and were immediately acceded to by both parties. Michael rose in a good humor, and the boys were of course. Loud was their talking of their deeds of valor, as they retired. One little fellow, about seven years old, and about three feet and a half high, jumped up, cracked his feet together, and exclaimed, "by gingo, Peet Jones, Bill Smith and *me* can hold any *Sinjin* that ever trod Georgy grit." By the way, the name of *St. John*, was always pronounced "*Sinjin*," by the common people of that day; and so it must have been by Lord Bolingbroke himself, else his friend Pope would never have addressed him in a line so unmusical as

"Awake my St. John, leave all meaner things."

Nor would Swift, the friend and companion of both, have written

" What *St. John's* skill in state affairs,
What Ormond's valor, Oxford's cares."—
*   *   *   *   *
" Where folly, pride, and faction sway,
Remote from *St. John*, Pope and Gray."

HALL.

THE "CHARMING CREATURE" AS A WIFE.

Y nephew, George Baldwin, was but ten years younger than myself. He was the son of a plain, practical, sensible farmer, who, without the advantages of a liberal education, had enriched his mind by study and observation, with a fund of useful knowledge, rarely possessed by those who move in his sphere of life.— His wife was one of the most lovely of women. She was pious, but not austere; cheerful, but not light; generous, but not prodigal; economical, but not close; hospitable, but not extravagant. In native powers of mind, she was every way my brother's equal—in acquirements, she was decidedly his superior.—To this I have his testimony, as well as my own; but it was impossible to discover in her conduct, any thing going to shew that she coincided with us in opinion. To have heard her converse, you would have supposed she did nothing but read—to have looked through the departments of her household, you would have supposed she never read. Every thing which lay within her little province, bore the impress of her own hand, or acknowledged her supervision. Order, neatness, and cleanliness prevailed every where. All provisions were given out with her own hands, and she could tell precisely the quantity of each article that it would require to serve a given number of persons, without stint or wasteful profusion. In the statistics of domestic economy, she was perfectly versed. She would tell you, with astonishing accuracy, how many pounds of cured bacon, you might expect from a given weight of fresh pork—How many

quarts of cream, a given quantity of milk would yield—
How much butter, so much cream—How much of each
article it would take to serve so many persons, a month or a
year. Supposing no change in the family, and she would tell
you to a day, when a given quantity of provisions of any
kind would be exhausted. She reduced to certain knowledge
every thing that could be; and she approximated to it as
nearly as possible, with those matters which could not be.
And yet she scolded less, and whipt less, than any mistress of
a family I ever saw. The reason is obvious. Every thing
under her care went on with perfect system. To each servant was allotted his or her respective duties; and to each
was assigned the time in which those duties were to be performed. During this time, she suffered them not to be interrupted, if it was possible to protect them from interruption.
Her children were permitted to give no orders to servants
but through her, until they reached the age at which they
were capable of regulating their orders by her rules. She
laid no plans to detect her servants in theft, but she took
great pains to convince them that they could not pilfer
without detection; and this did she, without betraying any
suspicions of their integrity. Thus, she would have her bis-
cuits uniformly of a size, and under the form of *instructions* to
her cook, she would show her precisely the quantity of flour
which it took to make so many biscuit. After all this, she exposed her servants to as few temptations as possible. She
never sent them to the larder unattended, if she could avoid
it; and never placed them under the watch of children. She
saw that they were well provided with every thing they
needed, and she indulged them in recreations when she
could. No service was required of them on the Sabbath,

further than to spread the table, and to attend it—a service which was lightened as much as possible, by having the provisions of that day very simple, and prepared the day before.

Such, but half described, were the father and mother of George Baldwin. He was their only son and eldest child; but he had two sisters, Mary and Martha; the first four, and the second six years younger than himself—a son next to George having died in infancy. The two eldest children inherited their names from their parents, and all of them grew up worthy of the stock from which they sprang.

George, having completed his education at Princeton, where he was graduated with great honor to himself, returned to Georgia, and commenced the study of the law. After studying a year, he was admitted to the bar, just after he had completed his one and twentieth year. I have been told by gentlemen who belong to this profession, that one year is too short a time for preparation for the intricacies of legal lore; and it may be so, but I never knew a young man acquit himself more creditably than George did, in his maiden speech.

He located himself in the city of ——, seventy miles from his father's residence; and after the lapse of three years, he counted up eight hundred dollars, as the net profits of his last year's practice. Reasonably calculating, that his receipts would annually increase for several years to come, having no expenses to encounter, except for his board and clothing, (for his father had furnished him with a complete library,) he now thought of taking to himself a helpmate. Hitherto he had led a very retired, studious life; but now he began to court the society of ladies.

About this time, Miss Evelina Caroline Smith returned to the city, from Philadelphia, where, after an absence of three years, she had completed her education. She was the only child of a wealthy, unlettered merchant, who, rather by good luck than good management, had amassed a fortune of about fifty thousand dollars—Mr. Smith, was one of those men, who conceived that all earthly greatness, and consequently, all earthly bliss, concentred in wealth. The consequence was inevitable. To the poor, he was haughty, supercilious and arrogant, and not unfrequently, wantonly insolent; to the rich he was friendly, kind, or obsequious, as their purses equalled or overmeasured his own. His wife was even below himself in moral stature: proud, loquacious, silly. Evelina was endowed by nature with a good mind, and, what her parents esteemed of infinitely more value, she was beautiful from her infancy to the time when I introduced her to the reader; which was just after she had completed her seventeenth year. Evelina's time, between her six and fourteenth year, had been chiefly employed, in learning from her father and mother what a perfect beauty she was, and what kind of gewgaws exhibited her beauty to the greatest advantage—how rich she would be; and "what havoc she would make of young men's hearts, by-and-by." In these instructive lectures, her parents sometimes found gratuitous help, from silly male and female visiters, who, purely to win favor from the parents, would expatiate on the perfections of "the lovely," "charming," "beautiful little creature," in her presence. The consequence was, that pride and vanity became, at an early age, the leading traits of the child's character; and admiration and flattery, the only food which she could relish. Her parents subjected themselves to the loss of her society for three years, while she was at school in Philadelphia, from no better motive, than to put her on an equality with Mr. B's and Mr. C's daughters—or rather, to imitate the examples of Messrs. B. & C., merchants of the same city, who were very rich.

While she was in Philadelphia, Evelina was well instructed. She was taught, in what female loveliness truly consists—the qualities which deservedly command the respect of the wise and good; and the deportment which ensures to a female, the admiration of all. But Evelina's mind had received a bias, from which these lessons could not relieve it; and the only effect of them upon her, was to make her an accomplished hypocrite, with all her other foibles. She improved her instructions, only to the gratification of her ruling passion. In music she made some proficiency, because she saw in it, a ready means of gaining admiration.

George Baldwin had formed a partial acquaintance with Mr. Smith, before the return of his daughter; but he rather shunned, than courted a closer intimacy. Smith, however, had entrusted George with some professional business, found him trust-worthy, and thought he saw in him, a man, who at no very distant day, was to become distinguished, for both wealth and talents; and upon a very short acquaintance, he took occasion to tell him, "that whoever married his daughter, should receive the next day, a check for twenty thousand dollars." "That'll do," continued he, "to start upon; and when I and the old woman drop off, she will get thirty more." This had an effect upon George directly opposite to that which it was designed to have.

Miss Smith had been at home about three weeks, and the whole town had sounded the praises of her beauty and accomplishments; but George had not seen her; though Mr. Smith had in the mean time given him several notes to collect, with each of which, he "wondered how it happened that two so much alike as himself and George, had never been more intimate; and hoped he would come over in a sociable way and see him often." About this time, however, George received a special invitation to a large tea-party, from Mr. and Mrs. Smith, which he could not with propriety reject, and accordingly he went. He was received at the door by Mr. Smith, announced upon entering the drawing-room, and conducted through a crowd of gentlemen to Miss Smith, to whom he was introduced with peculiar emphasis. He made his obeisance, and retired; for common politeness required him to bestow his attentions upon some of the many ladies in the room, who were neglected by the gentlemen, in their rivalship for a smile, or word from Miss Evelina. She was the admiration of all the gentlemen, and with the exception of two or three *young* ladies, who "thought her too affected," she was praised by all the ladies. In short, by nearly universal testimony, she was pronounced "*a charming creature.*"

An hour had elapsed before George found an opportunity of giving her those attentions, which, as a guest of the family, courtesy required from him. The opportunity was at length, however, furnished by herself. In circling round the room to entertain the company, she reached George, just as the seat next to him had been vacated. This she occupied, and a conversation ensued, with every word of which she gained upon his respect and esteem. Instead of finding her that gay, volatile, vain creature, whom he expected to find in the rich and beautiful daughter of Mr. and Mrs. Smith; he found her, a modest, sensible, unassuming girl, whose views upon all subjects, coincided precisely with his own.

"She yielded to the wishes of her parents, from a sense of duty, in giving and attending parties; but she always left them, under the conviction that the time spent at them was worse than wasted. It was really a luxury to her, to retire from the idle chit-chat of them, and to spend a few minutes in conversation with a male or female friend, who would consider it no disrespect to the company, to talk rationally upon such occasions. And yet, in conducting such conversations at such times, it was so difficult to avoid the appearance of pedantry, and to keep it from running into something too stiff or too grave for a social circle, that she really was afraid to court them." As to books, "she read but very few novels, though her ignorance of them often exposed her to some mortification; but she felt that her ignorance here, was a compliment to her taste and delicacy, which made ample amends for the mortifications to which it forced her occasionally to submit. With Hannah Moore, Mrs. Chapone, Bennett and other writers of the same class, she was very familiar;" (and she descanted upon the peculiar merits of each,) "But, after all, books were of small consequence to a lady, without those domestic virtues which enable her to blend superior usefulness with superior acquirements; and if learning, or usefulness must be forsaken, it had better be the first. Of music, she was extravagantly fond, and she presumed she ever would be; but she confessed, she had no taste for its modern refinements."

Thus she went on with the turns of the conversation, and as she caught George's views. It is true, she would occasionally drop a remark which did not harmonize exactly with these dulcet strains; and in her rambles over the world of science, she would sometimes seem at fault, where George thought she ought to have been perfectly at home; but he found a thousand charitable ways of accounting for all this; not one of which led to the idea, that she might have learned these diamond sentiments by rote, from the lips of her preceptress. Consequently they came with resistless force upon the citadel of George's heart, and in less than half an hour, overpowered it completely.

"Truly," thought George, "she is a charming creature! When was so much beauty ever blended with such unassuming manners, and such intellectual endowments! How wonderful, that the daughter of *Mr. and Mrs. Smith* should possess such accomplishments! How dull—with all her filial affection—how dull must be her life, under the parental roof! Not a companion, not a sympathetic feeling there! How sweet it would be to return from the toils of the Courts, to a bosom friend, so soft, so benevolent, so intelligent!"

Thus ran George's thoughts, as soon as Miss Smith had left him, to go in quest of new conquests. The effects of her short interview with him, soon became visible to every eye. His conversation lost its spirit—was interrupted by moody abstractions, and was sillier than it had ever been. George had a fine person, and for the first time in his life, he now set a value upon it. To exhibit it to the greatest advantage, he walked the room under various pretence; and when in his promenades he caught the eye of Miss Smith resting upon him, he assumed a more martial or theatric step, which made him look ridiculous at the time, and feel so immediately afterwards. In his listless journeyings, his attention was arrested by a beautiful cottage scene, at the foot of which glittered in golden letters,

"By Evelina Caroline Smith, of ———, Georgia."

This led him to another, and another, from the same pencil. Upon these he was gazing with a look and attitude the most complimentary to Miss Evelina that he could possibly assume, while the following remarks were going the rounds.

"Do you notice George Baldwin?"

"Oh yes! he's in for it—dead sir—good bye to bailwrits and *sassiperaris!*"

"Oh she's only put an *attachment* on him."

"Really, Miss Smith, it was too bad, to serve George Baldwin so cruelly!"

"Ah, sir, if reports are true, Mr. Baldwin is too fond of his books to think of any lady; much less of one, so unworthy of his attentions as I am."

George heard this—nestled a little—threw back his shoulders—placed his arms a kimbo, and looked at the picture with wonderful independence.

Then Miss Evelina was handed to the piano, and to a simple, beautiful air, she sang a well-written song, the burden of which was, an apology for love at first sight. This was wanton cruelty to an unresisting captive. To do her justice, however, her performance had not been equalled during the evening.

The company at length began to retire; and so long as a number remained sufficient to give him an apology for staying, George delayed his departure. The last group of ladies and gentlemen finally arose, and George commenced a fruitless search for his hat—fruitless, because he looked for it where he knew it was not to be found. But a servant was more successful, and brought it to him, just as he was giving up the search as hopeless, and commencing a conversation with Miss Smith, for the night.

"Why where did you find it?" said George, with seeming surprise and pleasure at the discovery.

"Out da, in de entry, sir, whay all de gentleman put da hats."

"Oh, I ought to have known that."

"*Good*-bye, Miss Evelina!" said George, throwing a melting eloquence into the first word, and reaching forth his hand.

"Good evening, Mr. Baldwin!" returned she, "I hope you will not be quite so great a stranger here as you have been. Pa has often wondered that you never visit him."—Here she relinquished his hand with a gentle, but sensible pressure, which might mean two or three things. Whatever was its meaning, it ran like nitrous oxide through every fibre of George's composition, and robbed him for a moment of his last ray of intellect.

"Believe me, Miss Smith," said he, as if he were opening a murder case, "believe me—there are fascinations about this hospitable home—in the delicate touches of the pencil which adorn it, and in the soft breathings of the piano, awaked by the hand which I have just relinquished, which will not permit me to delay, as heretofore, those visits which professional duty requires me to make to your kind parent, (your father,) a single moment beyond the time that his claims to my respects become absolute—Good evening, Miss Smith."

"Did ever mortal of common sense, talk and act so much like an arrant fool as I have this evening!" said George, as the veil of night fell upon the visions which had danced before his eyes, for the four preceding hours.

Though it was nearly twelve o'clock at night when he

reached his office, he could not sleep until he laid the adventures of the evening before his father and mother. The return mail brought him a letter from his parents, written by his mother's hand, which we regret we cannot give a place in this narrative. Suffice it to say, it was kind and affectionate, but entirely too cold for the temperature of George's feelings. It admitted the intrinsic excellence of Miss Smith's views and sentiments, but expressed serious apprehensions that her habits of life would prove an insuperable barrier to her ever putting them in full practice. "We all *admit*, my dear George," said the amiable writer, "the value of industry, economy—in short, of all the domestic and social virtues; but how small the number who *practice* them! Golden sentiments are to be picked up any where. In this age they are upon the lips of every body; but we do not find that they exert as great an influence upon the morals of society, as they did in the infancy of our Republic, when they were less talked of. For ourselves, we confess we prize the gentleman or lady who habitually practices one christian virtue, much higher, than we do the one who barely *lectures* eloquently, upon them all. But we are not so weak or so uncharitable as to suppose, that none who discourse fluently upon them, can possess them."

*   *   *   *   *   *

"The whole moral which we would deduce from the foregoing remarks, is, one which your own observation must have taught you a thousand times; that but little confidence is to be reposed in fine sentiments, which do not come recommended by the life and conduct of the person who retails them. And yet, familiar as you are with this truth, you certainly have more command over your judgment, than have most young men of your age, if you do not entirely forget it, the moment you hear such sentiments from the lips of '*a lady possessing strong personal attractions.*' There is a charm in beauty, which even philosophy is constrained to acknowledge; and which youth instinctively transfers to all the moral qualities of its possessor."

*   *   *   *   *   *

"When you come to know the elements of which connubial happiness is composed, you will be astonished to find, that with few exceptions, they are things which you now consider the veriest trifles imaginable. It is a happy ordination of Providence, that it should be so; for this brings matrimonial bliss within the reach of all classes of persons."

*   *   *   *   *   *   "Harmony of thought and feeling upon the little daily occurrences of life, congeniality of views and sentiments, between yourselves and your connexions on either side, similarity of habits and pursuits among your immediate relatives and friends, if not essential to nuptial bliss, are certainly its chief ingredients."   *

*   *   *   *   "Having pointed you to the sources of conjugal felicity, your own judgment will spare my trembling hand the painful duty of pointing you to those fountains of bitterness and woe—but I forget that I am representing your father as well as myself."———

George read the long letter, from which the foregoing extracts are taken, with deep interest, and with some alarm; but he was not in a situation to profit by his parents' counsels. He had visited Miss Smith repeatedly in the time he was waiting to hear from his parents; and though he had discovered many little foibles in her character, he found a ready apology, or an easy remedy for them all.

The lapse of a few months found them engaged; and George, the happiest mortal upon earth.

"And now, my dear Evelina," said he, as soon as they had interchanged their vows, "I go to render myself worthy of the honor you have conferred upon me. My studies, which love, doubt and anxiety have too long interrupted, shall now be renewed with redoubled intensity. My Evelina's interest being associated with all my labors, will turn them to pleasures; my honor, being hers, I shall court it with untiring zeal. She will therefore, excuse me, if my visits are not repeated in future, quite as often as they have been heretofore."

"What a'ready, Mr. Baldwin!" exclaimed she, weeping most beautifully.

"Why no, not for the world, if my dear Evelina says not! But I thought that—I flattered myself—I hoped—my Evelina would find a sufficient apology in the motive."

The little mistake was rectified in the course of an hour, and they parted more in raptures with each other than they had ever been.

George continued his visits as before, and in the mean time his business began to suffer from neglect, of which his clients occasionally reminded him, with all the frankness which one exhibits at seeing a love affair carried on with too much zeal, and at his expense. In truth George's heart had more than once entertained a wish, (for his lips dare not utter it,) that his charming Evelina's affection could come down to a hundred of Wedgewood, when the Circuit commenced, and give him a temporary respite.

The evening before he set out, he spent with his "charming Evelina" of course, and the interview closed, with a most melting scene; but I may not stop to describe it. Can-

dor constrains me to say, however, that George got over it
before he reached his office, which he entered, actually
whistling a merry tune.

He was at the second Court of the circuit, and had been
from home nearly a fortnight, when one of his friends addressed him, with—"I'll tell you what it is, Baldwin, you'd
better go home, or Dr. Bibb will cut you out. There have
been two or three parties in town, since you come away, at
all of which Miss Smith and Bibb were as thick as two pick-
pockets.—The whole town's talking about them. I heard a
young lady say to her, she'd tell you how she was carrying
on with Bibb, and she declared upon her word and honor,
(looking *killniferously* at Bibb,) that she only knew you as her
father's collecting attorney."

George reddened deeper and deeper at every word of
this; but passed it off with a hearty, hectic laugh.

It was on Thursday afternoon that he received this intelligence, and it met him forty miles from home, and twenty-
five from the next Court in order. Two of his cases were yet
undisposed of. Of these he gave hasty notes to one of his
brethren, in order to guide him, if he should be forced to
trial, but instructing him to continue them if he could. Having made these arrangements, Friday afternoon, at five
o'clock, found his jaded horse at his office-door. George tar-
ried here no longer than was necessary to change his appar-
el, and then he hastened to the habitation of his "charming
Evelina."

He was received at the door by a servant, who escorted
him to the drawing-room, and who, to heighten Evelina's
joy by surprise, instructed her maid to tell her, that there
was a *gentleman* in the drawing-room, who wished to see her.

Minute after minute rolled away, and she did not make her appearance. After he had been kept in suspense for nearly a quarter of an hour, she entered the room, dressed in bridal richness and taste.

"Why, is it you!" said she, rushing to him in transports: "I thought it was Dr. Bibb."

"And who is Dr. Bibb, Evelina?" said George.

"He's a young physician, with whom I had a partial acquaintance in Philadelphia, and who has just settled himself in this place. I want you to get acquainted with him, for he is one of the most interesting young gentlemen I ever knew in my life."

"No doubt I should be much pleased with him; but do you think he would feel *himself* much honored or improved by an acquaintance with '*your father's collecting attorney?*' "

"Why!—Is it possible that Rebecca Freeman has told you that! I never will speak to her again. I am the most persecuted being upon earth. I can say nothing, nor do nothing, no matter how innocent, which some one does not make a handle of to injure me."

Here Miss Evelina burst into tears, as usual; but there being a little passion mingled with her tears, on this occasion, her weeping was not quite as interesting as it had been before. It subdued George, however, and paved the way to a reconciliation. The obnoxious expression was explained, rather awkwardly, indeed, but satisfactorily; and Miss Freeman was acquitted of all blame.

Matters were just placed in this posture, when a servant arrived to inform George "that something was the matter with his horse, and Mr. Cox, (his landlord,) thought he was going to die."

George rose, and was hastening to the relief of his favorite of all quadrupeds, when Miss Smith burst in a very significant, but affected laugh.

"Why what is it amuses you so, Evelina?" inquired George, with some surprise.

"Oh nothing," said she; "I was only thinking how quick Mr. Baldwin forgets me, when his *horse* demands his attentions. I declare I'm right jealous of my rival."

"Go back, boy, and tell your master I can't come just now; but I'll thank him to do what he can for the poor animal."

Mr. Cox, upon receiving this intelligence, and learning the business which engrossed George's attention, left the horse to take care of himself; and he died just before George returned from Mr. Smith's.

These, and a thousand little annoyances, which we may not enumerate, urged upon George the importance of hastening the nuptials as speedily as possible.

Accordingly, by all the dangers, ills, alarms, and anxieties, which attend the hours of engagement, he pressed her to name the happy day within the coming month, when their hearts and their destinies should be inseparably united.

But "she could not think of getting married for two years yet to come—then, one year at least. At all events, she could not appoint a day until she consulted her dear Morgiana Cornelia Marsh, of Canaan, Vermont. Morgiana was her classmate, and at parting in Philadelphia, they had interchanged pledges that which ever got married first, should be waited upon by the other."

In vain did George endeavor to persuade her that this was a school-girl pledge, which Morgiana had already forgotten, and which she never would fulfil. His arguments only provoked a reproof of his unjust suspicions of the "American fair."

Finding his arguments here unavailing, he then entreated his "charming Evelina" to write immediately to Miss Marsh, to know when it would be agreeable to her to fulfil her promise.

Weeks rolled away before Miss Smith could be prevailed upon even to write the all-important letter. She despatched it at last, however; and George began to entertain hopes, that a few months would make the dear Evelina his own.

In the meantime his business fell in arrears, and his clients complained loudly against him. He was incessantly tortured with false rumors, of his cold and indifference towards Miss Smith, and of the light and disrespectful remarks which he had made upon her; but he was much more tortured by her unabated thirst for balls and parties of pleasure; her undiminished love of general admiration, and the unconcealed encouragement which she gave to the attentions of Dr. Bibb. The effect which these things had upon his temper was visible to all his friends. He became fretful, petulant, impatient and melancholy. Dr. Bibb proved, in truth, to be a most accomplished, intelligent gentleman; and was the man who, above all others, George would have selected for his friend and companion, had not the imprudences of Evelina transformed him into a rival. As things were, however, his accomplishments only embittered George's feelings towards him, provoked from George, cruel, misplaced and unnatural sarcasms, which the world placed to the account of jealousy, and in which George's conscience forced him to admit that the world did him nothing more nor less than sheer justice.

At length Miss Morgiana's letter arrived. It opened with

expressions of deep contrition that the writer "should have got married without giving her beloved Evelina an opportunity of fulfilling her promise; but really, after all, she was not to blame; for she did propose to write to her beloved Evelina to come on to Canaan; but Papa and Mr. Huntington, (her husband,) would not hear to it—Indeed, they both got almost vexed, that she should think of such a thing."   *   *   *   *   *   *   *   "But as soon as my beloved Evelina gets married, she must appoint a time at which we can meet at Philadelphia, with our husbands, and compare notes."   *   *   *   *   *   *   *   "I have a thousand secrets to tell you about married life; but I must reserve them till we meet. A thousand kisses to your dear George, for me; and tell him if I were not a married woman I should certainly fall in love with him, from your description of him."

"Well, I declare," said Evelina, as she folded up the letter, "I could not have believed that Morgiana would have served me so. I would have died before I would have treated her in the same way."

The great obstacle being now removed, the wedding night was fixed at the shortest time that it could be, to allow the necessary preparations; which was just three months ahead.

Before these three months rolled away, George became convinced that he had staked his earthly happiness upon the forlorn hope of reforming Miss Smith's errors, after marriage; but his sense of honor was too refined, to permit him to harbor a thought of breaking the engagement; and, indeed, so completely had he become enamored of her, that any perils seemed preferable to giving her up forever.

He kept his parents faithfully advised of all the incidents
of his love and courtship, and every letter which he for-
warded, went like a serpent into the Eden of peace over
which they presided. Their letters to him never came un-
embalmed in a mother's tears, and were never read without
the tender response which a mother's tears ever draws,
from the eyes of a truly affectionate son.

The night came, and George and Evelina were married.

A round of bridal parties succeeded, every one of which
served only to heighten George's alarms, and to depress his
spirits. He could not discover that marriage had abated, in
the smallest degree, his wife's love of general admiration
and flattery. The delight which she felt at the attentions of
the young gentlemen, was visible to more eyes than his; as
was plainly evinced by the throngs which attended her
wheresoever she moved. Occasionally their assiduities assumed a freedom, which was well calculated to alarm and
to inflame one whose notions of married life, were much less
refined than those which George had ever entertained; but
there was an apology for them, which he knew he would be
forced to admit, flimsy as it was, in truth; namely, "they
were only those special attentions which were due to the
queen of a bridal party." Another consideration forced him
to look in silence upon those liberties. *His wife* had taken no
offence at them. She either did not repel them at all, or she
repelled them in such a good humored way, that she encouraged, rather than prevented, the repetition of them.
For *him* therefore to have interposed, would have been considered an act of supererogation.

To the great delight of George, the parties ended; and
the young couple set out on a visit to LaGrange, the resi-

dence of George's parents. On their way thither, Evelina was secluded, of course, from the gaze of every person but her husband; and her attachment now became as much too ardent, as it had before been too cold. If, at their stages, he left her for a moment, she was piqued at his coldness, or distressed at his neglect. If he engaged in a conversation with an acquaintance or a stranger, he was sure to be interrupted by his wife's waiting-maid, Flora, with "Miss 'V'lina say, please go da, sir;" and when he went, he always found her in tears, or in a pet, at having been neglected so long by him, "when he knew she had no friend or companion to entertain her, but himself."

George had been long acquainted with the ladies of the houses at which they stopt. They all esteemed him, and were all anxious to be made acquainted with his wife; but she could not be drawn from her room, from the time she entered a house, until she rose to leave it. All her meals were taken in her room; and George was rebuked by her, because he would not follow her example. It was in vain that he reasoned with her upon the impropriety of changing his deportment to his old acquaintances immediately after his marriage. He stated to her, that the change would be attributed to pride—that he should lose a number of humble, but valuable acquaintances, which, to a professional gentleman, is no small loss. But "she could not understand that a gentleman is at liberty to neglect his wife, for 'humble, but valuable acquaintances.' "

When they reached LaGrange, they received as warm a welcome from George's parents, as parents, laboring under their apprehensions, could give; but Mary and Martha, having nothing to mar their pleasures, (for they had not been permitted to know the qualifications which George's last letters had annexed to his first,) received her with all the delight which the best hearts could feel, at welcoming to the family, in the character of a sister, the beautiful, amiable, accomplished, intelligent, wealthy, Miss Smith. In anticipation of her coming, the girls had brushed up their history, philosophy, geography, astronomy and botany, for her especial entertainment—or rather, that they might appear a little at home when their new sister should invite them to a ramble over the fields of science. The labor answered not its purpose, however; Evelina would neither invite, nor be invited to any such rambles.

The news of George's arrival at LaGrange with his wife, brought many of his rustic acquaintances to visit him. To many of them, George was as a son, or a brother, for he had been acquainted with them, from his earliest years, and he had a thousand times visited their habitations, with the freedom with which he entered his father's. They met him, therefore, with unrestrained familiarity, and treated his wife as a part of himself. George had endeavored to prepare her for the plain, blunt, but honest familiarities, of his early friends. He had assured her that however rude they might seem, they were perfectly innocent; nay, they were tokens of guileless friendship; for the natural disposition of plain, unlettered farmers, was to keep aloof from "the quality," as they called the people of the town, and that by as much as they overcame this disposition, by so much did they mean to be understood as evincing favor; but Evelina profited but little by his lessons.

The first visitor was old Mr. Dawson, who had dandled George on his knee a thousand times, and who, next to his father, was the sincerest male friend that George had living.

"Well, Georgy," said the old man, "and you've got married?"

"Yes, uncle Sammy; and here's my wife—what do you think of her?"

"Why she's a mighty pretty creater; but you'd better took my Nance. She'd 'ave made you another sort of wife, to this pretty little soft creater."

"I don't know sir," said Evelina, a little fiery, "how you can tell what sort of a wife a person will make, whom you never saw. And I presume Mr. Baldwin is old enough to choose for himself."

"Ah, well *now* I *know* he'd better 'ave took my Nance," said the old man, with a dry smile. "Georgy, my son, I'm afraid you've got yourself into bad business; but I wish you much happiness, my boy. Come, neighbor Baldwin, let's go take a look at your farm."

"Oh no," said old Mr. Baldwin, "we will not go till I make my daughter better acquainted with you. She is unused to our country manners, and therefore does not understand them. Evelina, my dear, Mr. Dawson is one of our best and kindest neighbors, and you and he must not break upon your first acquaintance. He was only joking George in what he said, and had no idea that you would take it seriously."

"Well, sir," said Evelina, "if Mr. Dawson will say that he did not intend to wound my feelings, I'm willing to forgive him."

"Oh, God love your pretty little soul of you," said the old man, "I did n't even know you had any feelings; but as to the *forgiving* part, why, that's neither here, nor there"— Here Evelina rose indignantly, and left the room.

"Well Georgy, my son," continued the old man, "I'm sorry your wife's so touchy! but *you* must n't forget old daddy Dawson. Come, my boy, to our house, like you used to, when you and Sammy, and Nancy, used to sit round the bowl of buttermilk under the big oak that covered Mammy Dawson's dairy. I always think of poor Sammy when I see you," (brushing a tear from his eye, with the back of his hand.) "I'm obliged to love you, you young dog; and I want to love your wife too, if she'd let me; but be that as it may, Sammy's playmate won't forget daddy Dawson, will he, George?"

George could only say "Never!" with a filling eye; and the old men set out for the fields.

Another Would "Buss Her" Because She Was George's Wife

Most of the neighbors who came to greet George upon his return to LaGrange shared Mr. Dawson's fate. One wanted to span Evelina's waist, for he declared "she was the littlest creater round the waist he ever *seed*." Another would "*buss her*, because she was George's wife, and because it was the first chance he ever had in all his life to buss 'the quality.' " A third proposed a swap of wives with George; and all made some remark too blunt for Evelina's refined ear. Having no tact for turning off these things playfully, and as little disposition to do so, she repelled them with a town dignity, which soon relieved her of these intrusions; and in less than a week, stopt the visits of George's first and warmest friends, to his father's house.

Her habits, views, and feelings, agreeing in nothing with the family in which she was placed, Evelina was unhappy herself, and made all around her unhappy. Her irregular hours of retiring and rising, her dilatoriness in attending her meals, her continued complaints of indisposition, deranged all the regulations of the family, and begat such confusion in the household, that even the elder Mrs. Baldwin occasionally lost her equanimity; so that when Evelina announced a week before the appointed time that she must return home, the intelligence was received with pleasure, rather than pain.

Upon their return home, George and his lady found a commodious dwelling, handsomely furnished for their reception. Mr. Smith presented him this in lieu of the check of which he had spoken, before the marriage of his daughter; and though the gift did not redeem the promise by $14,000, George was perfectly satisfied. Mrs. Smith added to the donation, her own cook and carriage-driver. Flora, the maid, had been considered Evelina's from her infancy. Nothing could have been more agreeable to George, than the news that greeted him on his arrival, that he was at liberty to name the day when he would conduct Evelina to his own house; for his last hope of happiness hung upon this last change of life. He allowed himself but two days after his return, to lay in his store of provisions; and on the third, at four in the afternoon, he led his wife to their mutual home.

"To this moment, my dear Evelina," said George, as they seated themselves in their own habitation, "to this moment have I looked forward for many months with the liveliest interest. I have often figured to myself the happy hours that we should enjoy under the common roof, and I hope the hour has arrived, when we will unite our endeavors to realize my fond anticipations. Let us then, upon the commencement of a new life, interchange our pledges, that we will each exert ourselves to promote the happiness of the other. In many respects, it must be acknowledged that our views and dispositions are different; but they will soon be assimilated by identity of interest, community of toil, and a frank and affectionate interchange of opinions, if we will but consent to submit some little sacrifices in the beginning, to attain this object. Now tell me, candidly and fearlessly, my Evelina, what would you have me be, and what would you have me do, to answer your largest wishes from your husband?"

"I would have you," said Evelina, "think more of me than all the world beside—I would have you the first lawyer in the State—I would have you overcome your dislike to such innocent amusements as tea-parties and balls—and I would have you take me to the Springs, or to New-York, or Philadelphia, every summer.—Now what would you have me do?"

"I would have you rise when I do—Regulate your servants with system—See that they perform their duties in the proper way, and the proper time—Let all provisions go through your hands, and devote your spare time to reading valuable works, painting, music, or any other improving employment, or innocent recreation. Be thus, and I '*will* think more of you than all the world beside;' 'I *will* be the first lawyer in the State,' and after a few years you *shall* visit the North, or the Springs every summer, if you desire it."

"Lord, if I do all these things you mention, I shall have no time for reading, music or painting."

"Yes you will. My mother"—

"Oh, for Lord's sake, Mr. Baldwin, hush talking about your mother. I'm sick and tired of hearing you talk of 'my mother' this, and 'my mother' that—And when I went to your house, I did'nt see that she got along a bit better than my mother—except in her cooking: and that was only because your mother cooked the meats, and your sisters made the pastry. I don't see the use of having servants, if one must do every thing herself."

"My sisters make the pastry, to be sure; because mother desires that they should learn how to do these things, that they may better superintend the doing of them, when they get married; and because she thinks such things should not pass through the hands of servants, when it can be avoided; but my mother never cooks."

"She does, for I saw her lifting off a pot myself."

"She does not"—

Here the entry of the cook stopt a controversy that was becoming rather warm for *the first evening at home*.

"I want the keys Miss 'V'lina, to get out supper," said the cook.

"There they are, *aunt** Clary," said Evelina; "try and have every thing very nice."

"My dear, I would n't send her to the provisions un-attended: every thing depends upon your commencing right"—

"Hush!" said Evelina, with some agitation, "I would n't have her hear you for the world. She'd be very angry if she thought we suspected her honesty. Ma always gave her up the keys, and she says she never detected her in a theft in all her life."

"Very well," said George, "we'll see."

After long waiting, the first supper made its appearance. It consisted of smoked tea, half-baked biscuit, butter, and sliced venison.

"Why," said Evelina, as she sipped her first cup of tea, "this tea seems to me to be smoked. Here, Flora, throw it out and make some more. Oh me! the biscuit an't done. Aunt Clary's made quite an unfortunate beginning. But I did 'nt want any supper—do you?"

"I can do without it," said George, coldly, "if you can."

"Well, let's not eat any, and that will be the very way to mortify aunt Clary, without making her mad. Tomorrow I'll laugh at her for cheating us out of our supper; and she wont do so any more. The old creature has very tender feelings."

"I'll starve for a week to save Clary's feelings," said George, "if you will only quit *aunting* her. How can you ex-pect her to treat you or your orders, with respect, when you treat her as your superior?"

* "Aunt" and "mauma," or "maum," its abbreviation, are terms of respect, com-monly used by children, to aged negroes. The first generally prevails in the up country, and the second on the sea-board.

"Well, really, I can't see any great harm in treating aged people with respect, even if their skins are black."

"I wish you had thought of that when you were talking to old Mr. Dawson. I should think he was entitled to as much respect, as an infernal black wench!"

This was the harshest expression that had ever escaped George's lips. Evelina could not stand it. She left the room, threw herself on a bed, and burst into tears.

In the course of the night the matter was adjusted.

The next morning George rose with the Sun, and he tried to prevail upon his wife to do the same; but "she could not see what was the use of her getting up so soon, just to set about doing nothing: and to silence all further importunities then and after, upon that score, she told him flatly she never would consent to rise at that hour."

At half after eight, she made her appearance; and breakfast came in. It consisted of muddy Coffee, hard-boiled eggs, and hard-burnt biscuit.

"Why, what has got into aunt Clary," said Evelina, "that she cooks so badly!"

"Why, we mortified her so much, my dear, by eating *no* supper;" said George, "and we have driven her to the opposite extreme. Let us now throw the breakfast upon her hands, except the coffee, and perhaps she'll be *mortified* back to a medium."

"That's very witty, indeed," said Evelina; "You must have learnt it from the amiable and accomplished Miss Nancy Dawson."

This was an allusion which George could not withstand; and he reddened to scarlet.

"Evelina," said he, "you are certainly the strangest being that I ever met with; you are more respectful to negroes than whites, and to every body else than your husband."

"Because," returned she, "negroes treat me with more respect than some whites; and every body else, with more respect than my husband."

George was reluctant to commence tightening the reins of discipline with his servants, for the first few weeks of his mastership: and, therefore, he bore in silence, but in anger, their idleness, their insolence, and their disgusting familiarities with his wife. He often visited the kitchen, unobserved, of nights; and almost always found it thronged with gay company, revelling in all the dainties of his closet, smoke-house, sideboard, and pantry. He communicated his discoveries to his wife, but she found no difficulty in accounting satisfactorily for all that he had seen. "Clary's husband had always supplied her with every thing she wanted. Flora had a hundred ways of getting money; and Billy, (the carriage-driver,) was always receiving little presents from her, and others."

At the end of three weeks *aunt* Clary announced that the barrel of flour was out.

"Now," said George, "I hope you are satisfied that it is upon *your* flour, and not upon her husband's, that *Aunt Clary* gives her entertainments."

"Why, law me!" said Evelina; "I think it has lasted wonderfully. You recollect Ma and Pa have been here most every day."

"Had they *boarded* with us," said George, "we could not have consumed a barrel of flour in three weeks."

In quick succession came the news that the tea, coffee, and sugar were out; all of which Evelina thought "had lasted wonderfully."

It would be useless to recount the daily differences of

George and his wife. In nothing could they agree; and the consequence was, that at the end of six weeks, they had come to downright quarrelling; through all which Evelina sought, and received the sympathy of Miss Flora and aunt Clary.

About this time the Superior Court commenced its session in the city; and a hundred like favors, received from the judge and the bar, imposed upon George the absolute necessity of giving a dinner to his brethren. He used every precaution to pass it off well. He gave his wife four days notice; he provided every thing himself, of the best that the town would afford; and he became all courtesy and affection to his wife, and all respect and cheerfulness to aunt Clary, in the interim. He promised all the servants a handsome present each, if they would acquit themselves well upon this occasion, and charged them all, over and over, to remember, that the time between two, and half past three, was all that the bar could allow to his entertainment; and consequently, dinner must be upon the table precisely at two.

The day came, and the company assembled. Evelina, attired like a queen, received them in the drawing-room; and all were delighted with her. All were cheerful, talkative and happy. Two o'clock came, and no dinner—A quarter after —and no dinner. The conversation began to flag a little. Half past two rolled round—and no dinner—Conversation sunk to temperate, and George rose to intemperate. Three quarters past two came—but no dinner—Conversation sunk to freezing, and George rose to fever heat.

At this interesting moment, while he was sauntering every way, George sauntered near his wife, who was deeply engaged in a conversation with his brother Paine, a grave, intelligent young man, and he detected her in the act of re-peating, *verbatim et literatim,* the pretty sentences which first subdued his heart.

"Good Lord!" muttered George to himself; "Jenkinson, in the Vicar of Wakefield, with his one sentence of learning, revived!"

He rushed out of the room, in order to enquire what de-layed dinner; and on leaving the dining-room, was met at the door by Flora, with two pale-blue, dry, boiled fowls; boiled almost to dismemberment, upon a dish large enough to contain a goodly sized shote; their legs sticking straight out, with a most undignified straddle, and bowing with a bewitching grace and elasticity to George, with every step that Flora made.

Behind her followed Billy, with a prodigious roast tur-key, upon a dish that was almost concealed by its contents, his legs extended like the fowls, the back and sides burnt to a crisp, and the breast raw. The old gentleman was hand-somely adorned with a large black twine necklace; and through a spacious window, that by chance or design the cook had left open, the light poured into his vacant cavity, gloriously.

George stood petrified at the sight; nor did he wake from his stupor of amazement until he was roused by a burnt round of beef, and a raw leg of mutton, making by him for the same port in which the fowls and turkey had been moored.

He rushed into the kitchen in a fury. "You infernal heif-er!" said he to aunt Clary; "what kind of cooking is this you're setting before my company?"

"Eh—Eh! Name o' God, Mas. George; how any body gwine cook ting good when you hurry 'em so?"

George looked for something to throw at her head; but fortunately found nothing.

He returned to the house, and found his wife entertaining the company with a never ending Sonata, on the piano.

Dinner was at length announced, and awful sight it was when full spread. George made as good apologies as he could; but his wife was not in the least disconcerted—Indeed, she seemed to assume an air of self-complaisance, at the profusion and richness which crowned her board.

The gentlemen ate but little, owing, as they said, to their having all eaten a very hearty breakfast that morning. George followed his guests to the Court House, craved a continuance of his cases for the evening, on the ground of indisposition; and it was granted, with an unaccountable display of sympathy. He returned home, and embarked in a quarrel with his wife, which lasted until Evelina's exhausted nature sunk to sleep under it, at three the next morning.

George's whole character now became completely revolutionized. Universal gloom overspread his countenance—He lost his spirits, his energy, his life, his temper, his everything ennobling; and he had just begun to surrender himself to the bottle, when an accident occurred which revived his hopes of happiness with his wife, and determined him to make one more effort to bring her into his views.

Mr. Smith, by an unfortunate investment in cotton, failed; and after a bungling attempt to secrete a few thousand dollars from his creditors, (for he knew George too well to claim his assistance in such a matter,) he was left without a dollar that he could call his own. Evelina and her parents all seemed as if they would go crazy under the misfortune; and George now assumed the most affectionate deportment to his wife, and the most soothing demeanor to her parents. The parents were completely won to him; and his wife, for once, seemed to feel towards him as she should. George availed himself of this moment to make another, and the last attempt, to reform her habits and sentiments.

"My dear Evelina," said he, "we have nothing now to look to, but our own exertions, for a support. This, and indeed affluence, lies within our reach, if we will but seek them in a proper way. You have only to use industry and care within doors, and I without, to place us in a very few years, above the frowns of fortune. We have only to consult each other's happiness, to make each other happy. Come then, my love, forgeting our disgraceful bickerings, let us now commence a new life. Believe me, there is no being on this earth, that my heart can love as it can you, if you will but claim its affections; and you know how to command them." Thus, at much greater length, and with much more tenderness, did George address her. His appeal had, for a season, its desired effect. Evelina rose with him, retired with him, read with him. She took charge of the keys, dealt out the stores with her own hand, visited the kitchen—in short, she became every thing George could wish or expect from one of her inexperience. Things immediately wore a new aspect. George became himself again. He recommenced his studies with redoubled assiduity. The community saw and delighted in the change, and the bar began to tremble at his giant strides in his profession.—But alas! his bliss was doomed to a short duration. Though Evelina saw, and felt, and acknowledged the advantages and blessings of her new course of conduct, she had to preserve it by struggle against nature; and at the end of three months, nature triumphed

over resolution, and she relapsed into her old habits.—
George now surrendered himself to drink, and to despair,
and died the drunkard's death. At another time, I may perhaps give the melancholy account of his ruin in detail; trac-
ing its consequences down to the moment at which I am now
writing. Should this time never arrive, let the fate of my
poor lost nephew, be a warning to mothers, against bringing up their daughters to be "CHARMING CREATURES."

BALDWIN.

THE GANDER PULLING.

IN the year 1798, I resided in the City of Augusta, and
upon visiting the Market-House, one morning in that
year, my attention was called to the following notice,
stuck upon one of the pillars of the building:

" *advurtysement.*"

"Thos woo wish To be inform heareof, is heareof notyfide that
"edwd. Prator will giv a gander pullin, jis this side of harisburg, on
"Satterday of thes pressents munth to All woo mout wish to partak
"tharof."

" e Prator, thos wishin to purtak
"will cum yearly, as the pullin will begin soon."

" e. p."

If I am asked, why "jis this side of harisburg" was selected for the promised feat, instead of the City of Augusta? I
answer from conjecture, but with some confidence, because,

the ground chosen, was near the central point, between four rival towns, the citizens of all which *"mout wish to partak tharof"*; namely, Augusta, Springfield, Harrisburg, and Campbellton—Not that each was the rival of all the others; but, that the first and the last were competitors, and each of the others backed the pretensions of its nearest neighbor. Harrisburg sided with Campbellton, *not because she had any interest in seeing the business of the two States centre upon the bank of the river, nearly opposite to her*; but because, like the "Union Democratic Republican Party of Georgia," she thought, after the adoption of the Federal Constitution, that the several towns of the confederacy should no longer be "separated" by the distinction of local party; but that laying down all former prejudices and jealousies, as a sacrifice on the altar of their country, they should become united in a *single body*, for the maintenance of those principles which they deemed essential to the *public welfare*."

Springfield, on the other hand, espoused the State Rights' creed. She admitted, that under the Federal compact, she ought to love the sister States very much; but that under the *Social Compact*, she ought to love her own state a little more; and she thought the two compacts perfectly reconcilable to each other. Instead of the towns of the several States, getting into *single bodies*, to preserve the *public welfare*, her doctrine was, that they should be kept in *separate bodies*, to preserve the *private welfare*. She admitted frankly, that living as she always had lived, right amidst gullies, vapours, fogs, creeks, and lagoons, she was wholly incapable of comprehending that expansive kind of benevolence, which taught her to love people whom she knew nothing about, as much as her next door neighbors and friends.—Until therefore, she should learn it from the practical operation of the Federal Compact, she would stick to the old-fashioned Scotch love, which she understood perfectly, and "go in" for Augusta, live or die, hit or miss, right or wrong. As in the days of Mr. Jefferson, the Springfield doctrines prevailed— Campbellton was literally *nullified;* in so much, that ten years ago, there was not a house left to mark the spot where once flourished this active, busy little village. Those who are curious to know where Springfield stood, at the time of which I am speaking, have only to take their position at the intersection of Broad and Marbury Streets, in the city of Augusta, and they will be in the very heart of old Springfield. Sixty steps West, and as many East of this position, will measure the whole length of this Jeffersonian Republican village, which never boasted of more than four dwelling-houses; and Broad-street, measures its width, if we exclude kitchens and stables. And, while upon this subject, since it has been predicted by a man, for whose opinions I entertain the profoundest respect,* (especially since the prediction,) that my writings will be read, with increased interest, a hundred years to come; and as I can see no good reason, if this be true, why they should not be read a thousand years hence, with more interest; I will take the liberty of dropping a word here, to the curious reader, of the year 1933. He will certainly wish to know the site of Harrisburg, (seeing it is doomed, at no distant period, to share the fate of Springfield,) and of Campbellton.

Supposing then, that if the great fire in Augusta, on the 3d of April, 1829, did not destroy that city, nothing will; I select this as a permanent object.

* The Editor of the "Hickory Nut."

In 1798, Campbell street was the western verge of Augusta, a limit to which it had advanced but a few years before, from Jackson street. Thence to Springfield, led a large road, —now built up on either side, and forming a continuation of Broad-street—This road was cut across obliquely, by a deep gully, the bed of which was an almost impassable bog, which entered the road, about one hundred yards below Collock street, on the South, and left it, about thirty yards below Collock street, on the North side of now Broad street. It was called Campbell's-Gully, from the name of the gentleman, through whose possessions, and near whose dwelling, it wound its way to the river. Following the direction of Broad-street, from Springfield, westward, 1347 yards, will bring you to Harrisburg; which had nothing to boast of over Springfield, but a warehouse, for the storage of tobacco, then the staple of Georgia.—Continue the same direction, 700 yards, then face to your right hand, and follow your nose directly across Savannah river, and upon ascending the opposite bank, you will be in the busiest part of Campbellton, in 1798. Between Harrisburg and Springfield, and 1143 yards from the latter, there runs a stream which may be perpetual. At the time just mentioned, it flowed between banks twelve or fourteen feet high, and was then called, as it still is, "Hawk's Gully."*

Now, Mr. Prator, like the most successful politician of the present day, was on all sides, in a doubtful contest; and accordingly he laid off his gander-pulling ground, on the nearest suitable unappropriated spot, to the centre point between Springfield and Harrisburg. This was between

* It took its name from an old man, by the name of Hawk, who lived in a log hut, on a small knoll, on the Eastern side of the gully, and about 100 yards South of the Harrisburg road.

Harrisburg and Hawk's Gully, to the south of the road, and embraced part of the road, but within 100 yards of Harrisburg.

When "*Satterday of thes presents munth*" rolled round, I determined to go to the gander-pulling. When I reached the spot, a considerable number of persons of different ages, sexes, sizes, and complexions, had collected from the rival towns, and the country around. But few females were there, however; and those few, were from the lowest walks of life.

A circular path of about forty yards diameter, had already been laid out; over which, from two posts about ten feet apart, stretched a rope, the middle of which was directly over the path. The rope hung loosely, so as to allow it, with the weight of a gander attached to it, to vibrate in an arc of four or five feet span, and so as to bring the breast of the gander, within barely easy reach of a man of middle stature, upon a horse of common size.

A hat was now handed to such as wished to enter the list; and they threw into it twenty-five cents each; this sum was the victor's prize.

The devoted gander was now produced; and Mr. Prator, having first tied his feet together, with a strong cord, proceeded to the *neck-greasing*. Abhorrent as it may be, to all who respect the tenderer relations of life, *Mrs.* Prator had actually prepared a gourd of *goose*-grease for this very purpose. For myself, when I saw Ned dip his hands into the grease, and commence stroking down the feathers, from breast to head, my thoughts took a melancholy turn—They dwelt in sadness upon the many conjugal felicities which had probably been shared between the *greasess* and the *greasee*.—I could see him as he stood by her side, through many a chilly day and cheerless night, when she was warming into life, the offspring of their mutual loves, and repelled, with chivalrous spirit, every invasion of the consecrated spot, which she had selected for her incubation. I could see him moving with patriarchal dignity, by the side of his loved one, at the head of a smiling, prattling group, the rich reward of their mutual care, to the luxuries of the meadow, or to the recreations of the pool. And now alas! an extract from the smoking sacrifice of his bosom friend, was desecrated to the unholy purpose of making his neck "a fit object" for Cruelty to reach "her quick, unerring fingers at." Ye friends of the sacred tie! judge what were my feelings, when in the midst of these reflections, the voice of James Prator thundered on mine ear, "Durn his old dodging soul; brother Ned! grease his neck till a fly can't light on it!"

Ned having fulfilled his brother Jim's request as well as he could, attached the victim of his cruelty to the rope, directly over the path. On each side of the gander, was stationed a man, whose office it was, to lash forward any horse which might linger there for a moment; for by the rules of the ring, all pulling was to be done at a brisk canter.

The word was now given for the competitors to mount and take their places on the ring. Eight appeared—Tall Zubley Zin, mounted upon Sally Spitfire; Arch Odum, mounted on Bull-and-Ingons (onions); Nathan Perdew, on Hell-cat; James Dickson, on Nigger; David Williams, on Gridiron; Fat John Fulger, on Slouch; Gorham Bostwick, on Gimblet; and Turner Hammond, on Possum.

"Come, *gentlemen*," said commandant Prator, "fall in! All of you git behind one another, sort o' in a row."

All came into the track very kindly, but Sally Spitfire, and Gridiron. The former, as soon as she saw a general movement of horses, took it for granted, there was mischief brewing, and because she could not tell where it lay, she concluded it lay every where, and therefore took fright at every thing.

Gridiron was a grave horse; but a suspicious eye which he cast to the right and left, wherever he moved, showed, that "he was wide awake," and that "nobody better not go fooling with him," as his owner sometimes used to say. He took a sober, but rather intense view of things; in so much, that in his contemplations, he passed over the track three times, before he could be prevailed upon to stop in it. He stopt, at last, however, and when he was made to understand, that this was all that was expected of him for the present, he surrendered his suspicions at once, with a countenance which seemed plainly to say, "Oh, if this is all you want, I've no objection to it."

It was long before Miss Spitfire could be prevailed upon to do the like.

"Get another horse; Zube," said one, "Sall will never do for a gander pullin."

"I won't," said Zube. "If she won't do, I'll make her do. I want a nag that goes off with a spring; so that when I get a hold, she'll cut the neck in two like a steel-trap."

At length Sally was rather flung than coaxed, into the track, directly ahead of Gridiron.

"Now gentlemen," said the Master of Ceremonies, "no man's to make a grab till all's been once round—and when the first man *are* got round, then the whole twist and tucking of you grab away, as you come under, ("Look here Jim

Fulger! you better not stand too close to that gander, I tell you,") one after another. "Now blaze away!" (the command for an onset of every kind, with people of this order.)

Off they went, Miss Sally delighted; for she now thought the whole parade would end in nothing more nor less, than her favorite amusement, a race. But Gridiron's visage pronounced this, the most nonsensical business, that ever a horse of sense was engaged in since the world began.

For the first three rounds, Zubly was wholly occupied in restraining Sally to her place, but he lost nothing by this, for the gander had escaped unhurt. On completing his third round, Zube reached forth his long arm, grabbed the gander by the neck, with a firmness, which seemed likely to defy *goose-grease*, and at the same instant, he involuntarily gave Sally a sudden check. She raised her head, which before had been kept nearly touching her leader's hocks, and for the first time, saw the gander in the act of descending upon her; at the same moment she received two pealing lashes from the whippers. The way she now broke, for Springfield, "is nothing to nobody." As Zube dashed down the road, the whole Circus raised a whoop after him. This started about twenty dogs, hounds, curs and pointers, in full chase of him, (for no man moved without his dog in those days.)—The dogs alarmed some belled cattle, which were grazing on Zube's path, just as he reached them; these joined him, with tails up, and a tremendous rattling. Just beyond these went three tobacco-rollers, at distances of fifty and a hundred yards apart; each of whom gave Zube a terrific whoop, scream, or yell, as he passed.

He went in and out of Hawk's Gully, like a trapball, and was in Springfield, "in less than no time." Here he was encouraged onward, by a new recruit of dogs; but they gave up the chase as hopeless, before they cleared the village. Just beyond Springfield, what should Sally encounter, but a flock of geese! the tribe to which she owed all her misfortunes. She stopt suddenly, and Zube went over her head with the last acquired velocity. He was up in a moment, and the activity with which he pursued Sally, satisfied every spectator that he was unhurt.

Gridiron, who had witnessed Miss Sally's treatment with astonishment and indignation, resolved not to pass between the posts, until the whole matter should be explained to his satisfaction. He therefore stopt short, and by very intelligible looks, demanded of the whippers, whether if he passed between them, he was to be treated as Miss Spitfire had been? The whippers gave him no satisfaction, and his rider signified by reiterated thumps of the heel, that he should go through, whether he would or not. Of these, however, Gridiron seemed to know nothing. In the midst of the conference, Gridiron's eye lit upon the oscillating gander, and every moment's survey of it begat in him a growing interest, as his slowly rising head, suppressed breath, and projected ears, plainly evinced. After a short examination, he heaved a sigh, and looked behind him, to see if the way was clear. It was plain that his mind was now made up; but to satisfy the world that he would do nothing rashly, he took another view, and then wheeled and went for Harrisburg, as if he had set in for a year's running. Nobody whooped at Gridiron, for all saw that his running was purely the result of philosophic deduction. The reader will not suppose all this consumed half the time which has been consumed in telling it, though it might have been so, without interrupting the

amusement; for Miss Spitfire's flight had completely suspended it for a time.

The remaining competitors now went on with the sport.
A few rounds showed plainly, that Odum or Bostwick
would be the victor; but which, no one could tell. Whenever either of them came round, the gander's neck was sure
of a severe wrench. Many a half pint of Jamaica was staked
upon them, besides other things. The poor gander withstood many a strong pull before his wailings ceased. At
length, however, they were hushed by Odum. Then came
Bostwick, and broke the neck. The next grasp of Odum, it
was thought, would bear away the head; but it did not—
Then Bostwick was sure of it—but he missed it. Now Odum
must surely have it—All is interest and animation—the
horses sweep round with redoubled speed—every eye is
upon Odum—his backers smiling, Bostwick's trembling—
To the rope he comes—lifts his hand—when, lo! Fat John
Fulger had borne it away the second before. All were astonished—all disappointed—and some were vexed a little; for
it was now clear, that "if it had n't o' been for his great fat
greasy paw," to use their own language, Odum would have
gained the victory. Others cursed, "that long-legged Zube
Zin, who was so high, he did n't know when his feet were
cold, for bringing such a nag as Sal' Spitfire, to a gander
pullen, for if he'd o' been in his place, it would o' flung Bostwick right where that *gourd* o' hog's *lard*, (Fulger) was."

Fulger's conduct was little calculated to reconcile them
to their disappointment.

"Come here Neddy Prater," said he, with a triumphant
smile, "let your Uncle Johnny put his potato stealer, (hand,)
into that hat, and tickle the chins of them *are* shiners a little!

Oh you little shining sons o' bitches! walk into your Mas' Johnny's pocket, and gingle, so as Arch Odum and Gory Bostwick may hear you!" You hear 'em Gory? *Boys*, don't pull with *men* any more. I've jist got my hand in; I wish I had a pond full o' ganders here now, jist to show how I could make their heads fly—Bet all I've won, you may hang three upon that rope, and I'll set Slouch at full speed, and take off the heads of all three, the first grab; two with my hands, and one with my teeth."

Thus he went on, but really, there was no boasting in all this; it was all fun, for John knew, and all were convinced that he knew, that his success, was entirely the result of accident. John was really "a good natured fellow," and his *cavorting* had an effect directly opposite to that which the reader would suppose it had—it reconciled all to their disappointment, save one. I except little Billy Mixen, of Spirit Creek; who had staked the net proceeds of six quarts of huckle-berries* upon Odom; which he had been long keeping for a safe bet. *He* could not be reconciled, until he fretted himself into a pretty little *piney*-woods fight, in which he got whipt; and then he went home perfectly satisfied. Fulger spent all his winnings with Prater in treats to the company—made most of them drunk, and thereby produced four Georgia *rotations;*† after which all parted good friends.

HALL.

---

* I give them their Georgia name. I should hardly be understood, if I called them *whortleberries.*

† I borrowed this term from Jim Inman, at the time.—"Why, Jim," said I to him just as he rose from a fight, "what have you been doing?" "Oh," said he, "nothing but taking a little *rotation* with Bob McManus."

THE BALL.

BEING on a visit to the city of ———, about ten years ago, my old friend, Jack De Bathle gave me an invitation to a ball, of which he was one of the managers. Jack had been the companion of my childhood, my boyhood, and my early manhood; and through many a merry dance had we hopt, and laughed, and tumbled down together, in the morning of life. Dancing was really, in those days, a merry making business. Except the minuet, which was introduced only to teach us the graces, and the congo, which was only to chase away the solemnities of the minuet, it was all a jovial, heart-stirring, foot-stirring amusement. We had none of your mathematical cotillons; none of your immodest waltzes; none of your detestable, disgusting gallopades. The *waltz* would have crimsoned the cheek of every young lady who attended a ball in my day; and had the gallopade been *commenced* in the ball room, it would have been *ended* in the street. I am happy to say that the waltz has met with but very little encouragement in Georgia as yet—the gallopade with none. Ye fair of my native land—Ye daughters of a modest race! blush them away from the soil, which your mothers honored by their example, and consecrated with their ashes. Born to woman's loftiest destinies, it ill becomes you to stoop from your high estate, to ape the indecencies of Europe's slaves. It is yours to command—not to obey. Let vice approach you in what form she may—as the handmaid of wit and talents, the mistress of courts, or the queen of fashion, fail not to meet her, with the frown of indignant virtue, and the flush of offended modesty. There is

a majesty in these, which has ever commanded her homage
—There is a loveliness in these, which will ever command
the admiration of the world. The interest which I feel, in
the character of the fair daughters of America, is my apology for this sober digression.

Though De Bathle is but two months younger than I am,
he still dances occasionally; and to this circumstance in
part, but more particularly to the circumstance of his being
a married man, is to be ascribed his appointment, of manager; the custom now being, to have one third, or one half
the managers, married men. This would be a great improvement on the management of balls in olden time, could
the married men only *manage* to keep out of the card-room.
Would they take the direction of the amusement into their
hands, their junior colleagues would then have an opportunity of sharing the pleasures of the evening, a privilege
which they seldom enjoy, as things are now conducted:
However, married men are not appointed with the expecta-
tion that they will perform the duties of the office; but to
quiet the scruples of some half dozen or more "*charming
creatures*," who, though they never fail to attend a ball, will
not condescend to do so, until they are perfectly satisfied it
is to be conducted with the utmost gravity, dignity, deco-
rum and propriety. For these assurances they look first to
"the face of the paper," (the ball-ticket) and if they do not
find on it a goodly number of responsible names, (such as
by reasonable presumption, are well broke to petticoat government,) they protest against it—tell a hundred amiable
little fibs, to conceal the cause of their opposition—torture
two or three beaux half to death with suspense, and finally
conclude to go "*just to keep from giving offence*." But if the en-

dorsers be "potent, grave and reverend seniors," schooled as aforesaid; why then, one difficulty at least is removed; for though it is well known, that these are "endorsers without recourse in the first instance," it is equally well known, that they may be ultimately made liable; for if the juniors fail to fulfil their engagements, a lady has nothing to do, but to walk into the card room, take a senior by the nape of the neck, lead him into the ball room, present her ticket with his name upon it, in the presence of the witnesses there assembled, and she is sure of ample satisfaction.

When De Bathle and I reached the ball room, a large number of gentlemen had already assembled. They all seemed cheerful and happy. Some walked in couples up and down the ball room, and talked with great volubility; but none of them understood a word that himself or his companion said.

"Ah, sir; how do you know that?"

Because the speakers showed plainly by their looks and actions, that their thoughts were running upon their own personal appearance, and upon the figure they would cut, before the ladies, when they should arrive; and not upon the subject of the discourse. And furthermore, their conversation was like that of one talking in his sleep,—without order, sense, or connexion. The hearer always made the speaker repeat in sentences and half sentences; often interrupting him with "what?" before he had proceeded three words in a remark; and then laughed affectedly, as though he saw in the senseless unfinished sentence, a most excellent joke. Then would come his reply, which could not be forced into connexion with a word that he had heard; and in the course of which, he was treated with precisely the civility which he had received. And yet they kept up the conversation with lively interest, as long as I listened to them.

Others employed themselves in commenting, good-humoredly, upon each other's dresses, and figure; while some took steps—awkwardly.

In the mean time the three junior managers met and agreed upon the parts which they were to perform. Herein I thought they were unfortunate. To Mr. Flirt, a bustling, fidgety, restless little man, about five feet two and a half inches high, was assigned the comparatively easy task of making out and distributing the numbers. Mr. Crouch, a good humored, sensible, but rather unpolished gentleman, undertook to attend the carriages, and to transport their precious treasures to the ball-room, where Mr. Dupree was to receive them, and see to their safe keeping, until the dancing commenced. The parts of the married men, up to the opening of the ball, was settled by common law. They were to keep a sharp look out, lend a helping hand in case of emergency, drink plenty of wine, see that other gentlemen, particularly strangers, did the same; and finally, to give any gentleman, who might have come to the ball, encumbered with a little loose change, an opportunity of relieving himself.

Things were thus arranged, Crouch standing with a group of gentlemen, of which I was one, in the entry leading to the ball room; when Mr. Flirt broke upon us as if the whole town was on fire, and all the ****** had risen, with "Good God, Crouch! There's Mrs. Mushy's carriage at the door, full of ladies, and not a manager there to receive them! I'll swear it is too bad!" "Horrible!" said Crouch; and away he went. But Mrs. Mushy, with Miss Feedle and Deedle, had reached the foot of the stairs unattended, be-

fore Crouch or even Flirt, who was considerably in advance
of him, met them. Mrs. Mushy, who was a lady of very full
habit, looked huffishly as Flirt took her hand, and Miss
Feedle, and Miss Deedle blushed sarcastically; Flirt made a
hundred apologies, and Crouch looked first at Mrs. Mushy,
then at Flirt, and tittered. "What a lovely figure Mrs.
Mushy is!" said he, as he turned off from delivering his
charge to Dupree. "Oh, Mr. Crouch," said Flirt, "if you
begin making your fun of the ladies a'ready, we'd better
break up the ball at once. By heaven, it's a shame." "Upon
my honor, Mr. Flirt," said Crouch, "I think she's beautiful.
I always liked a light and airy figure; particularly for a ball
room." By this time Dupree had joined us. Flirt left us, obviously in a pet; but we hardly missed him, before back he
rushed from the ball room, exclaiming, "Why, gracious
heavens, Dupree! there are those three ladies sitting in the
ball room, and not a gentleman in the room to entertain
them. Do go and introduce some of the gentlemen to them,
if you please." "Flugens!" said Dupree, "what an over-
sight!" and off he went for *entertainers*. After several ineffectual attempts, he at length prevailed on Mr. Noozle and
Mr. Boozle to be made acquainted with the ladies.

Mr. N. seated himself to the right of Mr. F., and Mr. B.
to the left of Miss D.; Mrs. M. occupying a seat between the
girls, and looking, for all the world, as if she thought—
"Well, this is the last ball I'll ever attend, unless it's a little
better managed." But the young ladies looked like a May
morning, as soon as the gentlemen approached. After a
pause of two minutes,

"It's a very pleasant evening," said Mr. Noozle to Miss
Feedle.

"Delightful," said Miss Feedle to Mr. Noozle.

"It's a delightful evening," said Miss Deedle to Mr. Boozle.

"Very pleasant," said Mr. Boozle to Miss Deedle.

"I thought there were some *married* managers of the ball," said Mrs. Mushy, emphatically. Here ensued a long pause.

"Are you fond of dancing?" said Mr. Noozle.

"Ah! what's that you say, Noozle?"—said Boozle; "you are not fond of dancing! Come, come, that'll never do. You tip the pigeon-wing too well for that."

"You quite misapprehend me, sir," returned Mr. Noozle. "Mine was not a declaration, touching in the remotest degree my personal predilections or antipathies, but a simple interrogatory to Miss Feedle. No sir; though I cannot lay claim to the proficiency of Noverre, in the saltant art, I am, nevertheless, extravagantly fond of dancing; too much so, I fear, for one who has but just commenced the *viginti lucubrationes annorum*, as that inimitable, and fascinating expositor of the elements of British jurisprudence, Sir William Blackstone, observes. To reach these high attainments in forensic"——

Here the young gentlemen were forced to resign their seats to a number of ladies, who now entered the ball room.

"What an intelligent young gentleman!" said Miss Feedle—"I declare I must set my cap for him."

"I think the other much the most interesting of the two," said Miss Deedle. "He's too affected, and too fond of showing off his learning. What did he call that 'inimitable expositor?' *Jinny Crashonis.*"

The seats were soon filled with ladies; almost all of whom, (except Mrs. Mushy,) entered the room in the same style, which seemed to have been strictly copied from the movement of the kildee. They took their seats, with precisely the motion with which the school-girls, in my younger days, used to make "*cheeses*," as they called them, with their frocks.

The musicians were all blacks, but neatly dressed. The band consisted of three performers on the violin, one on the clarionet, one on the tamborine, and one on the triangle.

The ladies ceased coming, and nothing seemed now wanting to begin the amusement, but the distribution of the numbers; but Mr. Flirt was running up and down stairs every minute after—no one knew what; and with great anxiety, no one knew why. He would enter the room, look the ladies all over, then down he would go; then return and go through the same evolutions. The band struck up a spirit-stirring tune, in which the tamborine player distinguished himself. For dignified complaisancy of countenance, under his own music, he rivalled Mr. Jenkins; and he performed the rattle-snake note with his middle finger, in a style which threw Miss Crump entirely in the shade. The band ceased, and the enquiry became general, "Why doesn't the drawing begin?" but Mr. Flirt still kept up his anxious movements.

"In the name of sense, Flirt," said Crouch, impatiently, as the little man was taking a third survey of the ladies, "what are you bobbing up and down stairs for? Why don't you distribute the tickets?"

"Oh," said Flirt, "it's early yet. Let's wait for Miss Gilt and Miss Rino. I know they're coming, for Mr. Posey, and Mr. Tulip told me they saw them dressed, and their carriages at the door, an hour ago."

"Blast Miss Gilt and Miss Rino!" returned Crouch. "Is the whole company to be kept waiting for them? Now, sir,

if the tickets are not handed round in three minutes, I'll announce to the company that Mr. Flirt will permit no dancing until Miss Gilt and Miss Rino, shall think proper to
honor us with their presence."

"Oh, zounds!" said Flirt, "I'm not waiting for them. I
thought it was too early to begin the drawing. It's quite un-
fashionable in New-York to commence drawing before 9
o'clock." (Miss R.'s father was computed at a cool hundred
and fifty, and Miss G.'s at a round hundred thousand.)

In a few minutes the tickets were distributed, and Mr.
Flirt proceeded to call, "No. 1—*First Cotillon*," with most
imposing majesty. Then numbers 2, 3, and 4, of the same;
then No. 1, of the second, and so on.

Five sets of cotillons could occupy the floor at a time; and
Flirt had just called No. 2, of the fifth, when Miss Rino entered the room, and immediately afterwards Miss Gilt. Flirt
had put two supernumerary tickets in the hat, in anticipation of their coming; and forgetting every thing else, he suspended the calling, and rushed to deliver them, as soon as
the ladies made their appearance.

He went to Miss Rino first, as she entered first; but she
was obviously piqued at seeing the sets on the floor before
her arrival. She refused to take a number; declaring, (very
sweetly,) that she left home with no idea of dancing. Flirt
insisted, earnestly and prettily, upon her taking a number;
but she hesitated, looked in the hat, then looked at Flirt be-
witchingly, and declared she did not wish to dance.

In the mean time Miss Gilt began to feel herself slighted,
and she said, in a pretty audible tone, "as for her part, she
would like very well to draw a number if she could be permitted to do so." Several gentlemen who had gathered

around her, hastened to Flirt to remind him of the indignity which he was offering to Miss Gilt; but before they reached him, Miss Rino drew No. 3, of the fifth cotillon from the hat.

Unfortunately, Crouch's patience had worn out, just before Miss R. made up her mind to take a ticket; and he took the office which Flirt had abdicated. He called No. 3 twice; but the call was not responded to. He then called No. 4, when Miss Jones appeared, and took her place. He next called No. 1, of the sixth set, when a lady appeared, which completed the cotillon. The last lady had but just taken her place, when Miss Rino, led on by Mr. Noozle, advanced, and announced that her's was No. 3, of the fifth set. Miss Jones was instinctively retiring from the august presence of Miss Rino, when she was stopped by Crouch, with "Keep your place, Miss Jones, I think you are entitled to it."

"Is'nt this No. 3, of the fifth cotillon?" said Miss Rino, holding out her ticket to Mr. Crouch.

"Yes, Miss," said Crouch, "but I think it has forfeited its place. Indeed, I do not think it was even drawn, when Miss Jones took her place."

This drew from Miss Rino the expression of countenance, which immediately precedes a sneeze.

"Upon every principle of equity and justice," said Mr. Boozle, "Miss Rino is entitled to"—

"Music!" said Crouch.

"Hands round!" said the fiddler; and the whole band struck into something like "The Dead March."

"This matter shall not end here," said Noozle, as he led Miss Rino back to her seat.

"Oh, Mr. Noozle," returned Miss Rino, "don't think any

thing of it. I declare I had not the least wish in the world to dance. Surely you would not object to any thing the *polite* and *accomplished Mr. Crouch* would do!"

Noozle walked the floor in portentous abstraction— wiped his face with terrific emphasis—and knocked his hair back with the slap belligerent.

The ladies who were not dancing became alarmed and sedate: (Miss Gilt excepted;) the gentlemen collected in groups, and carried on an animated conversation. As all but myself, who could give a correct version of the affair, were engaged in the dance, the Noozle party had gained over to their side most of the company present, before the dance ended. After various enquiries, rumors and corrections, the company generally settled down upon the following statement, as confirmed by the joint testimony of Rino, Flirt and Noozle.

"Crouch had an old spite against Miss Rino, for nothing at all—Began cursing and abusing her because she was not the first lady in the room—Refused to wait two minutes for her arrival—As soon as he saw her enter the ball room, usurped Mr. Flirt's appointment, and commenced calling the numbers on purpose to cut her out. She, seeing his object, snatched up a number, and rushed to her place; but it was occupied by Miss Jones; who seeing the superiority of her claims, offered to give way; and was actually retiring, when Crouch seized her by the arm, jerked her back, and said, "*Keep your place, Miss! You're entitled to it, if Miss Rino has got the number; and you shall have it.*" And when Mr. Noozle was pleading with him just to look at Miss Rino's ticket, he just turned upon his heel, and called for the music. This was all reported to Crouch, as confirmed by the trio before mentioned. He pronounced it all an infamous lie, from beginning to end, and was with difficulty restrained from going immediately after Flirt, to pick him up, as he said, and wear him out upon Noozle.

As soon as the first cotillon ended, the Crouch party began to gain ground; but not without warm words between several gentlemen, and a general depression of spirits through the company.

The dancing of the ladies was, with few exceptions, much after the same fashion. I found not the least difficulty in resolving it into the three motions, of a turkey-cock strutting, a sparrow-hawk lighting, and a duck walking. Let the reader suppose a lady beginning a strut at her own place, and ending it (precisely as does the turkey-cock,) three feet nearer the gentleman opposite her; then giving three sparrow-hawk bobs, and then waddling back to her place like a duck; and he will have a pretty correct idea of their dancing. Not that the three movements were blended at every turn of the dance; but that one or more of the three answered to every turn. The strut prevailed most in ballancing; the bobs, when ballanced to; and the waddle, when going round. To all this, Mrs. Mushy was an exception. When she danced, every particle of her danced, in spite of herself.

There was as little variety in the gentlemen's dancing as there was in the ladies'. Any one who has seen a gentleman clean mud off his shoes on a door mat, has seen nearly all of it; the principal difference being, that some scraped with a pull of the foot, some with a push, and some with both.

"I suppose," said I to a gentleman, "they take no steps because the music will not admit of them?"

"Oh no," said he; "It's quite ungenteel to take steps." I

thought of the wag's remarks about Miss Crump's music. "If this be their *dancing*," thought I, "what must their *mourning* be!"

A splendid supper was prepared at twelve o'clock; and the young ladies ate almonds, raisins, apples, oranges, jelly, sillabub, custard, candy, sugar-plums, kisses and cake, as if they had been owing them an old grudge. But the married gentlemen did not come up to supper.

"And how did the quarrel end?"

"Oh; I had like to have forgot the denouement of the quarrel."

A correspondence opened the next morning between the parties, in which Noozle was diffuse, and Crouch laconic. They once came this near an amicable adjustment of the difference. Noozle's second, (for the fashion is, for the principals to get into quarrels, and for the seconds to get them out,) agreed, if Crouch would strike the word "it," out of one of his letters, his friend would be perfectly satisfied.

Mr. Crouch's second admitted that the removal of the word would not change the sense of the letter the least; but that Mr. Crouch having put his life and character in his hands, he felt bound to protect them with the most scrupulous fidelity; he could not therefore consent to expunge the objectionable word, unless the challenge were withdrawn. To show, however, his reluctance to the shedding of blood; and to acquit his friend, in the eyes of the public, of all blame, he would take it upon himself to say, that if Mr. Noozle would withdraw his objections to the "t" Mr. Crouch should expunge the "i." This proposition was rejected; but in return, it was submitted, that if Mr. Crouch would expunge the "t" the "i" might remain. To which it was replied, that the alteration would convert the whole sentence into nonsense; making it read "*i is*," instead of "*it is*," &c. Here the seconds separated, and soon after the principals met; and Crouch shot Noozle, in due form, and according to the latest fashion, through the knees. I went to see him after he had received his wound; and poor fellow, he suffered dreadful tortures. So much, said I, for a young lady's lingering from a ball an hour too long, in order to make herself conspicuous.

BALDWIN.

THE MOTHER AND HER CHILD.

WHENCE comes the gibberish which is almost invariably used by mothers and nurses, to infants? Take for example the following, which will answer the two-fold purpose of illustrating my idea, and of exhibiting one of the peculiarities of the age.

A few days ago, I called to spend an hour in the afternoon, with Mr. Slang, whose wife is the mother of a child about eight months old.

While I was there, the child in the nurse's arms, in an adjoining room, began to cry.

"You, Rose," said Mrs. Slang, "quiet that child!" Rose walked it, and sang to it; but it did not hush.

"You, Rose! if you do not quiet that child, I lay I make you."

"I is tried, ma'am," said Rose, "an' he would'nt get hushed"—(*Child cries louder.*)

"Fetch him here to me, you good for nothing hussy you. What's the matter with him?" reaching out her arms to receive him.

"I dun know ma'am."

"Nhei—nhun—nho—nha'am!" (*mocking and grinning at Rose.*)

As Rose delivered the child, she gave visible signs of dodging, just as the child left her arms; and, that she might not be disappointed, Mrs. Slang gave her a box: in which there seemed to be no anger mixed at all; and which Rose received *as a matter of course*, without even changing countenance under it.

"Da den!" said Mrs. Slang, "come elong e muddy (mother). Did nassy Yosey, (Rose,) pague muddy thweety chilluns? (children)"—pressing the child to her bosom, and rocking it backward and forward tenderly. "Muddins will whippy ole nassy Yosey. Ah! you old uggy Yosey," (*knocking at Rose playfully.*) "Da den; muddy did wippy bad Yosey."

(*Child continues crying.*)

"Why what upon earth ails the child? Rose, you've hurt this child, somehow or other!"

"No m'm, 'cla' I didn't—I was jis sitt'n down dar in the rock'n chair long side o' Miss Nancy's bureau, an' want doin' nothin' 't all to him, jis playin' wid him, and he jis begin to cry heself, when nobody wa'n't doin' nothin' 't all to him, and nobody wa'nt in dar nuther sept jis me and him, and I was"—

"Nhing—nhing—nhing—and I expect you hit his head against the bureau."

"Let Muddy see where ole bad Yosey knocky heady 'gin de bureaus. Muddy *will* see," taking off the child's cap, and finding nothing.

(*Child cries on.*)

"Muddy's baby was hongry. Dat was what ails muddy's darling, thsweety ones. Was cho hongry, an' nobody would givy litty darling any sings 't all for eaty?" (*loosing her frock bosom.*) "No, nobody would gim thsweety ones any sings fo' eat 't all"—(*offers the breast to the child, who rejects it, rolls over, kicks, and screams worse than ever.*)

"Hush! you little brat! I believe it's nothin in the world but crossness. Hush! (*shaking it,*) hush I tell you." (*Child cries to the* NE PLUS ULTRA.)

"Why surely a pin must stick the child.—Yes, was e bad pin did ticky chilluns. Let muddy see where de uggy pin did ticky dear prettous creter"—(*examining*)—"Why no, it isn't a pin. Why what can be the matter with the child! It must have the cholic surely. Rose, go bring me the paragoric off the mantle-piece.—Yes, muddy's baby did hab e tolic. Dat was what did ail muddy's prettous darly baby." (*Pressing it to her bosom and rocking it. Child cries on.*)

Rose brought the paragoric, handed it, dodged, and got her expectations realized as before.

"Now go bring me the sugar, and some water."

Rose brought them, and delivered both without the customary reward; for at that instant, the child being laid perfectly still on the lap, hushed.

The paragoric was administered, and the child received it with only a whimper now and then. As soon as it received the medicine, the mother raised it up and it began to cry.

"Why Lord help my soul, what's the matter with the child! what have you done to him, you little hussy?" (*rising and walking towards Rose.*)

" 'Cla' Missis, I eint done nothin' 't all—was jis sittin' down da by Miss Nancy's bu—"

"You lie, you slut," (*hitting her a passing slap,*) "I know you've hurt him. Hush, my baby," (*singing the Coquet,*) don't you cry, your sweet-heart will come by'm'by; da, de dum dum dum day, da de dum diddle dum dum day."

(*Child cries on.*)

"Lord help my soul and body, what can be the matter with my baby!" (*tears coming in her own eyes.*) "Something's the matter with it; I know it is." (*Laying the child on her lap, and feeling its arms, to see whether it flinched at the touch of any particular part.*) But the child cried less while she was feeling it than before.

"Yes, dat was it; wanted litty arms yubb'd. Mud will yub its sweet little arms."

(*Child begins again.*)

"What upon earth can make my baby cry so!" rising and walking to the window. (*Stops at the window, and the child hushes.*)

"Yes, dat was it: did want to look out 'e windys. See the petty chickens. O-o-o-h! Look, at, the beauty, rooster!! Yonder's old aunt Betty! See old aunt Betty, pickin' up chips. Yes, ole aunt Betty, pickin' up chip fo' bake bicky, (biscuit) fo' good chilluns. Good aunt Betty fo' make bicky fo' sweet baby's supper."

(*Child begins again.*)

"Hoo-o-o! see de windy!" (*knocking on the window. Child screams.*)

"You Rose, what have you done to this child! You little hussy you, if you don't tell me how you hurt him, I'll whip you as long as I can find you."

"Missis I 'cla I never done noth'n' 't all to him. I was jis sett'n' down da by Miss Nancy's bu—"

"If you say '*Miss Nancy's bureau*' to me again, I'll stuff Miss Nancy's bureau down your throat, you little lying slut. I'm just as sure you've hurt him, as if I'd seen you. How did you hurt him?"

Here Rose was reduced to a *non plus;* for, upon the peril of having a bureau stuffed down her throat, she dare not repeat the oft-told tale, and she knew no other. She therefore stood mute.

"Julia," said Mr. Slang, "bring the child to me, and let me see if I can discover the cause of his crying."

Mr. Slang took the child, and commenced a careful examination of it. He removed its cap, and beginning at the crown of its head, he extended the search slowly and cautiously downward, accompanying the eye with the touch of the finger. He had not proceeded far in this way, before he discovered in the right ear of the child, a small feather, the cause, of course, of all its wailing. The cause removed, the child soon changed its tears to smiles, greatly to the delight of all, and to none more than to Rose.

BALDWIN.

THE DEBATING SOCIETY.

THE following is not strictly a "*Georgia Scene;*" but as Georgians were the chief actors in it, it may perhaps be introduced, with propriety, in these sketches.

About three and twenty years ago, at the celebrated school in W——n, was formed a Debating Society, composed of young gentlemen between the ages of seventeen and twenty-two. Of the number were two, who, rather from an uncommon volubility, than from any superior gifts or acquirements, which they possessed over their associates, were by common consent, placed at the head of the fraternity.—At least this was true of one of them: the other certainly had higher claims to his distinction. He was a man of the highest order of intellect, who, though he has since been known throughout the Union, as one of the ablest speakers in the country, seems to me to have added but little to his powers in debate, since he passed his twenty-second year. The name of the first, was Longworth; and McDermot was the name of the last. They were congenial spirits, warm friends, and classmates, at the time of which I am speaking.

It was a rule of the Society, that every member should speak upon the subjects chosen for discussion, or pay a fine; and as all the members valued the little stock of change, with which they were furnished, more than they did their reputation for oratory; not a fine had been imposed for a breach of this rule, from the organization of the society to this time.

The subjects for discussion, were proposed by the members, and selected by the President, whose prerogative it

was also to arrange the speakers on either side, at his pleasure; though in selecting the subjects, he was influenced not
a little, by the members who gave their opinions freely of
those which were offered.

It was just as the time was approaching, when most of the
members were to leave the society, some for college, and
some for the busy scenes of life, that McDermot went to
share his classmate's bed for a night. In the course of the
evening's conversation, the society came upon the tapis.
"Mac," said Longworth, "would'nt we have rare sport, if
we could impose a subject upon the society, which has no
sense in it, and hear the members speak upon it?"

"Zounds," said McDermot, "it would be the finest fun in
the world. Let's try it at all events—we can lose nothing by
the experiment."

A sheet of foolscap was immediately divided between
them, and they industriously commenced the difficult task
of framing sentences, which should possess the *form* of a de-
bateable question, without a particle of the *substance.*—After
an hour's toil, they at length exhibited the fruits of their
labor, and after some reflection, and much laughing, they
selected, from about thirty subjects proposed, the following,
as most likely to be received by the society:

"WHETHER AT PUBLIC ELECTIONS, SHOULD THE VOTES OF
FACTION PREDOMINATE BY INTERNAL SUGGESTIONS OR THE
BIAS OF JURISPRUDENCE.?"

Longworth was to propose it to the society, and McDermot was to advocate its adoption.—As they had every reason to suppose, from the practice of the past, that they
would be placed at the head of the list of disputants, and on
opposite sides, it was agreed between them, in case the ex-

periment should succeed, that they would write off, and interchange their speeches, in order that each might quote literally from the other, and thus *seem* at least, to understand each other.

The day at length came for the triumph or defeat of the project; and several accidental circumstances conspired to crown it with success. The society had entirely exhausted their subjects; the discussion of the day had been protracted to an unusual length, and the horns of the several boarding-houses began to sound, just as it ended. It was at this auspicious moment, that Longworth rose, and proposed his subject. It was caught at with rapture by McDermot, as being decidedly the best, that had ever been submitted; and he wondered that none of the members had ever thought of it before.

It was no sooner proposed, than several members exclaimed, that they did not understand it; and demanded an explanation from the mover. Longworth replied, that there was no time then for explanations, but that either himself or Mr. McDermot would explain it, at any other time.

Upon the credit of the *maker* and *endorser*, the subject was accepted; and under pretence of economising time, (but really to avoid a repetition of the question,) Longworth kindly offered to record it, for the Secretary. This labor ended, he announced that he was prepared for the arrangement of the disputants.

"Put yourself," said the President, "on the affirmative, and Mr. McDermot on the negative."

"The subject," said Longworth, "cannot well be resolved into an affirmative and negative. It consists more properly, of two conflicting affirmatives: I have therefore drawn out the heads, under which the speakers are to be arranged thus:

Internal Suggestions.
Bias of Jurisprudence.

Then put yourself Internal Suggestions—Mr. McDermot the other side, Mr. Craig on your side—Mr. Pentigall the other side," and so on.

McDermot and Longworth now determined that they would not be seen by any other member of the society during the succeeding week, except at times when explanations could not be asked, or when they were too busy to give them. Consequently, the week passed away, without any explanations; and the members were summoned to dispose of the important subject, with no other lights upon it than those which they could collect from its terms. When they assembled, there was manifest alarm on the countenances of all but two of them.

The Society was opened in due form, and Mr. Longworth was called on to open the debate. He rose and proceeded as follows:

"*Mr. President*—The subject selected for this day's discussion, is one of vast importance, pervading the profound depths of psychology, and embracing within its comprehensive range, all that is interesting in morals, government, law and politics. But, sir, I shall not follow it through all its interesting and diversified ramifications; but endeavor to deduce from it those great and fundamental principles, which have direct bearing, upon the antagonist positions of the disputants; confining myself more immediately to its psychological influence, when exerted, especially upon the *votes of faction:* for here is the point upon which the question mainly turns. In the next place, I shall consider the effects of those 'suggestions' emphatically termed '*internal*' when applied to the same subject. And in the third place, I shall compare these effects, with 'the bias of jurisprudence,' considered as the only resort in times of popular excitement —for these are supposed to exist by the very terms of the question.

"The first head of this arrangement, and indeed the whole subject of dispute, has already been disposed of by this society. We have discussed the question, 'are there any innate maxims?' and with that subject and this, there is such an intimate affinity, that it is impossible to disunite them, without prostrating the vital energies of both, and introducing the wildest disorder and confusion, where, by the very nature of things, there exists the most harmonious co-incidences, and the most happy and euphonic congeniali-ties. Here then might I rest, Mr. President, upon the decision of this society, with perfect confidence. But, sir, I am not forced to rely upon the inseparable affinities of the two questions, for success in this dispute, obvious as they must be to every reflecting mind. All history, ancient and modern, furnish examples corroborative of the views which I have taken of this deeply interesting subject.—By what means did the renowned poets, philosophers, orators and statesmen of antiquity, gain their immortality? Whence did Milton, Shakspeare, Newton, Locke, Watts, Paley, Burke, Chatham, Pitt, Fox, and a host of others whom I might name, pluck their never-fading laurels! I answer boldly, and without the fear of contradiction, that, though they all reached the temple of fame by different routes, they all passed through the broad vista of '*internal suggestions*.' The same may be said of Jefferson, Madison, and many other distinguished personages of our own country.

"I challenge the gentlemen on the other side to produce examples like these in support of their cause."

Mr. Longworth pressed these profound and logical views to a length to which our limits will not permit us to follow him, and which the reader's patience would hardly bear, if they would. Perhaps, however, he will bear with us, while we give the conclusion of Mr. Longworth's remarks: as it was here, that he put forth all his strength:

"*Mr. President*—Let the bias of jurisprudence predominate, and how is it possible, (considering it merely as extending to those impulses which may with propriety be termed a *bias*,) how is it possible, for a government to exist, whose object is the public good! The marble-hearted marauder might seize the throne of civil authority, and hurl into thraldom the votaries of rational liberty. Virtue, justice and all the nobler principles of human nature, would wither away under the pestilential breath of political faction, and an unnerved constitution, be left to the sport of demagogue and parasite.—Crash after crash, would be heard in quick succession, as the strong pillars of the republic give way, and Despotism would shout in hellish triumph amidst the crumbling ruins—Anarchy would wave her bloody sceptre over the devoted land, and the blood-hounds of civil war, would lap the crimson gore of our most worthy citizens. The shrieks of women, and the screams of children, would be drowned amidst the clash of swords, and the cannon's peal: and Liberty, mantling her face from the horrid scene, would spread her golden-tinted pinions, and wing her flight to some far distant land, never again to re-visit our peaceful shores. In vain should we then sigh for the beatific reign of those 'suggestions' which I am proud to acknowledge as peculiarly and exclusively 'internal.' "

Mr. McDermot rose promptly at the call of the President, and proceeded as follows:

"*Mr. President*—If I listened unmoved to the very labored appeal to the passions, which has just been made, it was not because I am insensible to the powers of eloquence; but because I happen to be blessed with the small measure of sense, which is necessary, to distinguish true eloquence from the wild ravings of an unbridled imagination. Grave and solemn appeals, when ill-timed and misplaced, are apt to excite ridicule; hence it was, that I detected myself more than once, in open laughter, during the most pathetic parts of Mr. Longworth's argument, if so it can be called.* In the midst of 'crashing pillars,' 'crumbling ruins,' 'shouting despotism,' 'screaming women,' and 'flying Liberty,' the question was perpetually recurring to me, 'what has all this to do with the subject of dispute?' I will not follow the example of that gentleman—It shall be my endeavor to clear away the mist which he has thrown around the subject, and to place it before the society, in a clear, intelligible point of view: for I must say, that though his speech '*bears strong marks of the pen*,' (sarcastically,) it has but few marks of sober reflection. Some of it, I confess, is very intelligible and very plausible; but most of it, I boldly assert, no man living can comprehend. I mention this, for the edification of that gentleman—(who is usually clear and forcible,) to teach him, that he is most successful when he labors least.

---

* This was extemporaneous, and well conceived; for Mr. McDermot had not played his part with becoming gravity.

"Mr. President: The gentleman, in opening the debate, stated that the question was one of vast importance; pervading the profound depths of *psychology*, and embracing, within its ample range, the whole circle of arts and sciences. And really, sir, he has verified his statement; for he has extended it over the whole moral and physical world. But, Mr. President, I take leave to differ from the gentleman, at the very threshhold of his remarks. The subject is one which is confined within very narrow limits. It extends no further than to the elective franchise, and is not even commensurate with this important privilege; for it stops short at the *vote of faction*. In this point of light, the subject comes within the grasp of the most common intellect; it is plain, simple, natural and intelligible. Thus viewing it, Mr. President, where does the gentleman find in it, or in all nature besides, the original of the dismal picture which he has presented to the society? It loses all its interest, and becomes supremely ridiculous. Having thus, Mr. President, divested the subject of all obscurity—having reduced it to those few elements, with which we are all familiar; I proceed to make a few deductions from the premises, which seem to me inevitable, and decisive of the question. I lay it down as a self-evident proposition, that faction in all its forms, is hideous; and I maintain, with equal confidence, that it never has been nor ever will be, restrained by those suggestions, which the gentleman '*emphatically terms internal.*' No, sir, nothing short of the bias, and the very strong bias too, of jurisprudence, or the potent energies of the sword, can restrain it. But, sir, I shall here, perhaps, be asked, whether there is not a very wide difference between a turbulent, lawless action, and the *vote* of faction? Most unquestionably there is; and to this distinction I shall presently advert, and demonstrably prove that it is a distinction, which makes altogether in our favor."

Thus did Mr. McDermot continue to dissect and expose his adversary's argument, in the most clear, conclusive and masterly manner, at considerable length. But we cannot deal more favorably by him, than we have dealt by Mr. Longworth. We must, therefore, dismiss him, after we shall have given the reader his concluding remarks. They were as follows:

"Let us now suppose Mr. Longworth's principles brought to the test of experiment. Let us suppose his language addressed to all mankind—'We close the temples of justice as useless; we burn our codes of laws as worthless; and we substitute in their places, the more valuable restraints of *internal suggestions*. Thieves, invade not your neighbor's property: if you do, you will be arraigned before the august tribunal of *conscience*. Robbers, stay your lawless hand; or you will be visited with the tremendous penalties of *psychology*. Murderers, spare the blood of your fellow creatures; you will be exposed to the excrutiating tortures of *inate maxims—when it shall be discovered that there are any*. Mr. President, could there be a broader license to crime than this? Could a better plan be devised for dissolving the bands of civil society? It requires not the gift of prophecy, to foresee the consequences, of these novel and monstrous principles. The strong would tyrannize over the weak; the poor would plunder the rich; the servant would rise above the master; the drones of society would fatten upon the hard earnings of the industrious —Indeed, sir, industry would soon desert the land; for it would have neither reward nor encouragement. Commerce would cease; the arts and sciences would languish; all the sacred relations would be dissolved, and scenes of havoc, dissolution and death ensue, such as never before visited the world, and such as never will visit it, until mankind learn to repose their destinies upon 'those suggestions, *emphatically termed internal.*'—From all these evils there is a secure retreat behind the brazen wall of the 'bias of jurisprudence.' "

The gentleman who was next called on to engage in the debate, was John Craig; a gentleman of good hard sense, but who was utterly incompetent to say a word upon a subject which he did not understand. He proceeded thus:

"*Mr. President*—When this subject was proposed, I candidly confessed I did not understand it, and I was informed by Mr. Longworth and Mr. McDermot, that either of them would explain it, at any leisure moment. But, sir, they seem to have taken very good care, from that time to this, to have no leisure moment. I have inquired of both of them, repeatedly for an explanation; but they were always too busy to talk about it. Well, sir, as it was proposed by Mr. Longworth, I thought he would certainly explain it in his speech; but I understood no more of his speech than I did of the subject. Well, sir, I thought I should certainly learn something from Mr. McDermot; especially as he promised at the commencement of his speech to clear away the mist that Mr. Longworth had thrown about the subject, and to place it in a clear, intelligible point of light. But, sir, the only difference between his speech and Mr. Longworth's, is, that it was not quite as flighty as Mr. Longworth's. I could n't understand head nor tail of it. At one time they seemed to argue the question, as if it were this: 'Is it better to have law or no law?' At another, as though it was, 'should fac-

tion be governed by law, or be left to their own consciences?'
But most of the time they argued it, as if it were, just what it
seems to be—a sentence without sense or meaning. But, sir,
I suppose its obscurity is owing to my dullness of apprehen-
sion—for they appeared to argue it with great earnestness
and feeling, as if they understood it.

"I shall put my interpretation upon it, Mr. President,
and argue it accordingly.

" 'WHETHER AT PUBLIC ELECTIONS'—that is, for members
of Congress, members of the Legislature, &c. 'SHOULD THE
VOTES *of faction*'—I don't know what *'faction'* has got to do
with it; and therefore I shall throw it out. 'SHOULD THE
VOTES PREDOMINATE, BY INTERNAL SUGGESTIONS OR THE BIAS'
—I don't know what the *article* is put in here for. It seems to
me, it ought to be, *be* BIASED *by* 'jurisprudence' or law—In
short, Mr. President, I understand the question to be,
should a man vote as he pleases, or should the law say how
he should vote?"

Here Mr. Longworth rose and observed, that though
Mr. Craig was on his side, he felt it due to their adversaries,
to state, that this was not a true exposition of the subject.
This exposition settled the question at once on his side; for
nobody would, for a moment, contend, that *the law* should
declare how men should vote. Unless it be confined to the
vote *of faction* and *the* bias of jurisprudence, it was no subject
at all. To all this Mr. McDermot signified his unqualified
approbation; and seemed pleased with the candor of his op-
ponent.

"Well," said Mr. Craig, "I thought it was impossible
that any one should propose such a question as that to the
society; but will Mr. Longworth tell us, if it does not mean

that, what does it mean? for I don't see what great change is made in it by his explanation."

Mr. Longworth replied, that if the remarks which he had just made, and his argument, had not fully explained the subject to Mr. Craig, he feared it would be out of his power to explain it.

"Then," said Mr. Craig, "I'll pay my fine, for I don't understand a word of it."

The next one summoned to the debate was Mr. Pentigall. Mr. Pentigall was one of those who would never acknowledge his ignorance of any thing, which any person else understood; and that Longworth and McDermot were both masters of the subject, was clear, both from their fluency and seriousness. He therefore determined to understand it, at all hazards.—Consequently he rose at the President's command, with considerable self-confidence. I regret, however, that it is impossible to commit Mr. Pentigall's *manner* to paper, without which, his remarks lose nearly all their interest. He was a tall, handsome man; a little theatric in his manner, rapid in his delivery, and singular in his pronunciation. He gave the *e* and *i,* of our language, the sound of *u*— at least his peculiar intonations of voice, seemed to give them that sound; and his rapidity of utterance seemed to change the termination, "*tion*" into "*ah.*" With all his peculiarities, however, he was a fine fellow. If he was ambitious, he was not invidious, and he possessed an amicable disposition. He proceeded as follows:

"*Mr. President*—This internal suggestion which has been so eloquently discussed by Mr. Longworth, and the bias of jurisprudence which has been so ably advocated by Mr. McDermot—hem!—Mr. President, in order to fix the line of demarkation between—ah—the internal suggestion and the bias of jurisprudence—Mr. President, I think, sir, that —ah—the subject must be confined to the *vote of faction*, and *the* bias of jurisprudence."

Here Mr. Pentigall clapt his right hand to his forehead, as though he had that moment heard some overpowering news; and after maintaining this position for about the space of ten seconds, he slowly withdrew his hand, gave his head a slight inclination to the right, raised his eyes to the President as if just awakening from a trance, and with a voice of the most hopeless despair, concluded with "I don't understand the subject, Muster Prusidunt."

The rest of the members on both sides submitted to be fined rather than attempt the knotty subject; but by common consent, the penal rule was dispensed with. Nothing now remained to close the exercises, but the decision of the Chair.

The President, John Nuble, was a young man, not unlike Craig in his turn of mind; though he possessed an intellect a little more sprightly than Craig's.—His decision was short.

"Gentlemen," said he, "I do not understand the subject. This," continued he (pulling out his knife, and pointing to the silvered or *cross* side of it) "is 'Internal Suggestions.' And this" (pointing to the other, or *pile* side) "is 'Bias of Jurisprudence':" so saying, he threw up his knife, and upon its fall, determined that 'Internal Suggestions' had got it; and ordered the decision to be registered accordingly.

It is worthy of note, that in their zeal to accomplish their purpose, Longworth and McDermot forgot to destroy the lists of subjects, from which they had selected the one so often mentioned; and one of these lists containing the subject discussed, with a number more like it, was picked up by Mr. Craig, who made a public exhibition of it, threatening to arraign the conspirators before the society, for a contempt. But, as the parting hour was at hand, he overlooked it with the rest of the brotherhood, and often laughed heartily at the trick.

HALL.

*THE MILITIA COMPANY DRILL.**

I HAPPENED, not long since, to be present at the muster of a captain's company, in a remote part of one of the counties; and as no general description could convey an accurate idea of the achievements of that day, I must be permitted to go a little into detail, as well as my recollection will serve me.

The men had been notified to meet at nine o'clock, "armed and equipped as the law directs;" that is to say, with a gun and cartridge box at least, but as directed by the law of the United States, "with a good firelock, a sufficient bayonet and belt, and a pouch with a box to contain no less than twenty-four sufficient cartridges of powder and ball."

At twelve, about one third, perhaps one half, of the men had collected, and an inspector's return of the number

* This is from the pen of a friend, who has kindly permitted me to place it among the "*Georgia Scenes.*" It was taken from the life, and published about twenty years ago.— *The Author.*

present, and of their arms, would have stood nearly thus: 1 captain, 1 lieutenant, ensign, none; fifers, none; privates, present 24; ditto, absent 40; guns, 14; gunlocks, 12; ramrods, 10; rifle pouches, 3; bayonets, none; belts, none; spare flints, none; cartridges, none; horsewhips, walking canes and umbrellas, 10. A little before one, the captain, whom I shall distinguish by the name of Clodpole, gave directions for forming the line of parade. In obedience to this order, one of the sergeants, whose lungs had long supplied the place of a drum and fife, placed himself in front of the house, and began to ball with great vehemence, "All Captain Clodpole's company parade here! Come GENTLEMEN, parade here!" says he—"all you that has n't got guns fall into the lower *eend*." He might have bawled till this time, with as little success as the syrens sung to Ulysses, had he not changed his post to a neighboring shade. There he was immediately joined by all who were then at leisure; the others were at that time engaged as parties or spectators at a game of fives, and could not just then attend. However, in less than half an hour the game was finished, and the captain enabled to form his company, and proceed in the duties of the day.

"*Look to the right and dress!*"

They were soon, by the help of the non-commissioned officers, placed in a straight line; but, as every man was anxious to see how the rest stood, those on the wings pressed forward for that purpose, till the whole line assumed nearly the form of a crescent.

"Why, look at 'em," says the captain; "why, gentlemen, you are all a crooking in at both *eends*, so that you will get on to me bye and bye! Come, gentlemen, *dress, dress!*"

Militia Drill

This was accordingly done; but, impelled by the same motives as before, they soon resumed their former figure, and so they were permitted to remain.

"Now, gentlemen," says the captain, "I am going to carry you through the *revolutions* of the manual exercise, and I want you, gentlemen, if you please, to pay particular attention to the word of command, just exactly as I give it out to you. I hope you will have a little patience, gentlemen, if you please, and if I should be agoing wrong, I will be much obliged to any of you, gentlemen, to put me right again, for I mean all for the best, and I hope you will excuse me if you please. And one thing, gentlemen, I caution you against, in particular—and that is this—not to make any *mistakes* if you can possibly help it; and the best way to do this, will be to do all the motions right at first; and that will help us to get along so much the faster; and I will try to have it over as soon as possible.—Come boys, come to a shoulder.

"*Poise, foolk!**

"*Cock, foolk!* Very handsomely done.

"*Take aim!*

"*Ram down catridge!* No! No! *Fire!* I recollect now that firing comes next after taking aim, according to Steuben; but, with your permission, gentlemen, I'll *read* the words of command just exactly as they are printed in the book, and then I shall be sure to be right." "Oh yes! read it Captain, read it"! (exclaimed twenty voices at once;) "that will save time."

" '*Tention the whole!* Please to observe, gentlemen, that at the word "fire!" you must fire; that is, if any of your guns are *loaden'd*, you must not shoot in *yearnest*, but only make pretence like; and you, gentlemen fellow soldiers, who's armed with nothing but sticks, riding switches and corn stalks, need n't go through the firings, but stand as you are, and keep yourselves to yourselves.

"*Half cock, foolk!* Very well done.

"*S, h, e, t*, (spelling) *Shet pan!* That too would have been handsomely done, if you had'nt handled cartridge instead of shetting pan; but I suppose you was n't noticing.—Now 'tention one and all, gentlemen, and do that motion again.

"*Shet pan!* Very good, very well indeed; you did that motion equal to any old soldier—you improve astonishingly.

"*Handle cartridge!* Pretty well, considering you done it wrong end foremost, as if you took the cartridge out of your mouth, and bit off the twist with the cartridge box.

"*Draw rammer!* Those who have no rammers to their guns need not draw, but only make the motion; it will do just as well, and save a great deal of time.

"*Return rammer!* Very well again—But that would have

---

* A contraction and corruption of "Firelock." Thus: "Firelock," "f'lock," "foolk."

been done, I think, with greater expertness, if you had performed the motion with a little more dexterity.

"*S, h, o, u, l—Shoulder foolk!* Very handsomely done indeed! Put your guns on the other shoulder, gentlemen.

"*Order foolk!* Not quite so well, gentlemen—not quite altogether; but perhaps I did not speak loud enough for you to hear me all at once. Try once more, if you please. I hope you will be patient, gentlemen; we will soon be through.

"*Order foolk!* Handsomely done, gentlemen!—Very handsome done! and altogether too, except that one half of you were a *leetle* too soon, and the other half a *leetle* too late.

"In laying down your guns, gentlemen, take care to lay the locks up and the other side down.

"*'Tention the whole! Ground foolk!* Very well.

"*Charge bayonet!*" (*Some of the men*)—"That can't be, Captain—pray look again; for how can we charge bayonet without our guns?"

(*Captain.*) "I don't know as to that, but I know I'm right, for here 'tis printed in the book; c, h, a, r—yes, *charge bayonet*, that's right, that's the word, if I know how to read. Come, gentlemen, do pray charge bayonet! Charge, I say! —Why don't you charge? Do you think it aint so? Do you think I have lived to this time o' day, and don't know what charge bayonet is? Here, come here, you may see for yourselves; it's plain as the nose on your fa—Stop—stay—no— halt! no! Faith I'm wrong! I turned over two leaves at once. I beg your pardon, we will not stay out long; and we'll have something to drink as soon as we have done. Come, boys, get up off the stumps and logs and take up your guns, we'll soon be done: excuse me if you please.

"*Fix Bayonet!*

"*Advance arms!* Very well done; turn the stocks of your guns in front, gentlemen, and that will bring the barrels behind; hold them straight up and down if you please; let go with your left, and take hold with your right hand below the guard. Steuben says the gun should be held, p, e, r, *pertic'lar*—yes, you must always mind and hold your guns very pertic'lar. Now boys, 'tention the whole!

"*Present arms!* Very handsomely done! only hold your gun over t'other knee—t'other hand up—turn your hands round a little and raise them up higher—draw t'other foot back—now you are nearly right—very well done.

"Gentlemen, we come now to the *revolutions*. Men, you have all got into a sort of snarl, as I may say; how did you get all into such a higglet pigglety?"

The fact was, the shade had moved considerably to the eastward, and had exposed the right wing of these hardy veterans to a galling fire of the sun. Being poorly provided with umbrellas at this end of the line, they found it convenient to follow the shade, and in huddling to the left for this purpose, they changed the figure of their line from that of a crescent to one which more nearly resembled a pair of pothooks.

"Come, gentlemen," (says the captain,) "spread yourselves out again in a straight line; and let us get into the wheelings and other matters as soon as possible."

But this was strenuously opposed by the soldiers.—They objected going into the *revolutions* at all, inasmuch as the weather was extremely hot, and they had already been kept in the field upwards of three quarters of an hour. They reminded the captain of his repeated promise to be as short as he possibly could, and it was clear he could dispense with all this same wheeling and flourishing, if he chose. They were already very thirsty, and if he would not dismiss them, they declared they would go off without dismission, and get something to drink, and he might fine them if that would do him any good; they were able to pay their fine, but would not go without drink to please any body; and they swore they would never vote for another captain who wished to be so unreasonably strict.

The captain behaved with great spirit upon the occasion, and a smart colloquy ensued; when at length becoming exasperated to the last degree, he roundly asserted that no soldier ought ever to *think hard* of the orders of his officer; and, finally, he went so far as to say that he did not think any gentleman on that ground had any just cause to be offended with him. The dispute was finally settled by the captain sending for some grog for their present accommodation, and agreeing to omit reading the military law, and the performance of all the manœuvres, except two or three such easy and simple ones as could be performed within the compass of the shade. After they had drank their grog, and had "spread themselves," they were divided into platoons.

" '*Tention the whole!—To the right wheel!*" Each man faced to the right about.

"Why, gentlemen, I did not mean for every man to stand still and turn himself *na'*trally right round; but when I told you to wheel to the right, I intended you to wheel round to the right as it were. Please to try again, gentlemen; every right hand man must stand fast, and only the others turn round."

In the previous part of the exercise, it had, for the purpose of sizing, been necessary to denominate every second person a "right hand man." A very natural consequence was, that on the present occasion those right hand men maintained their position, all the intermediate ones facing about as before.

"Why, look at 'em now!" exclaimed the captain, in extreme vexation—"I'll be d——d if you understand a word I say. Excuse me, gentlemen, it *rayly* seems as if you could not come at it exactly. In wheeling to the right, the right hand *eend* of the platoon stands fast, and the other *eend* comes round like a swingletree. Those on the outside must march faster than those on the inside. You certainly must understand me now, gentlemen; and please to try it once more."

In this they were a little more successful.

" *'Tention the whole! To the left—left, no—right—that is, the left—I mean the right—left wheel, march!*"

In this, he was strictly obeyed; some wheeling to the right, some to the left, and some to the right-left, or both ways.

"*Stop! halt!* Let us try it again! I could not just then tell my right hand from left! You must excuse me, if you please —experience makes perfect, as the saying is. Long as I have served, I find something new to learn every day; but all's one for that. Now, gentlemen, do that motion once more."

By the help of a non-commissioned officer in front of each platoon, they wheeled this time with considerable regularity.

"Now, boys, you must try to wheel by divisions; and there is one thing in particular which I have to request of you, gentlemen, and that is, not to make any blunder in your wheeling. You must mind and keep at a wheeling distance, and not talk in the ranks, nor get out of fix again; for

I want you to do this motion well, and not to make any blunder now.

"'*Tention the whole! By divisions, to the right wheel, march!*"

In doing this, it seemed as if Bedlam had broke loose: every man took the command. "Not so fast on the right!—Slow now?—Haul down those umbrellas!—Faster on the left!—Keep back a little there!—Don't *scrouge* so!—Hold up your gun Sam!—Go faster there!—faster! Who trod on my ————? d——n your huffs!—Keep back! Stop us, Captain —do stop us! Go faster there! I've lost my shoe! Get up again, Ned! Halt! halt! halt!—Stop, gentlemen! stop! stop!"

By this time they had got into utter and inextricable confusion and so I left them.

TIMOTHY CRABSHAW.

THE TURF.

"COME," said my friend Baldwin to me, a few months ago, "let us go to the turf."

"No," said I, "I take no interest in its amusements."

"Nor do I," rejoined he; "but I visit it to acquire a knowledge of the human character, as it exhibits itself in the various scenes of life, and with the hope of turning the knowledge thus acquired, to some good account. I am the more desirous that you should accompany me," continued he, "because, as one pair of eyes and ears cannot catch all that passes, within a scene so spacious, I shall lose many instructing, interesting, or amusing incidents, without the assistance of a friend; and therefore I wish to enlist your services."

"Well," said I, "with this view, I will accompany you."

We went; and the following is the result of our joint observations:

We went early, when as yet no one had reached the ground but those who occupied the booths for the purpose of traffic. It was not long, however, before crowds of persons of all ages, sexes, conditions and complexions, were seen moving towards the booths; some on foot, some on horseback, some in gigs, some in carriages, some in carts, and some in wagons. The carriages, (generally filled with well dressed làdies,) arranged themselves about thirty or forty

Hurrying to the Races

paces from the starting point, towards the centre of the turf. Around these, circled many young gentlemen, each riding his prettiest, whipping, spurring, and curbing his horse into the most engaging antics, and giving visible token that he thought every eye from the carriages was on him, and every heart overpowered by his horsemanship. As many more plied between the booths and carriages, bearing messages, rumors, apples, oranges, raisins, lemonade, and *punch.*

"But surely no lady drank the punch!"

"Yes, three of them did; and if I know what large swallows mean, they loved it too—but they did'nt drink long. The ladies ought to be informed, however, that a countryman passing them, observed, 'the way *them* women love punch is nothing to nobody!' "

The gentlemen generally collected about the booths, and employed themselves in loud talking and drinking. Here I saw Maj. Close, who two hours before declared he had not enough to pay a poor woman for the making of the vest he had on, treat a large company to a dollar bowl of punch; and, ten minutes after, I saw the same man stake fifty dollars on the race. I saw another gentleman do the same, who, four days before, permitted his endorser to lift his note in bank, for one hundred dollars, which note the endorser still held. But, thought I, the way these gentlemen treat their creditors, "is nothing to nobody." One thing I remarked upon this occasion, which should not be passed in silence. I saw many gentlemen drink *spirits* upon the turf, whom I never saw taste it any where else—some, because it seemed fashionable; and some, because they would bet nothing but a glass of toddy, or a bowl of punch, and having bet it, they must help drink it.

I had been employed, perhaps three quarters of an hour, in making observations upon the scene which was before me, when I observed a group of negroes and boys enter one of the gates of the turf, following with much seeming interest, a horse which was led by an aged black, by whose side walked a little negro boy about thirteen years of age, dressed in pink, throughout. I had no doubt but that the horse was one which was entered for the day's running; and as I was desirous of seeing all the competitors before the race, I advanced to meet him apart from the crowd. As soon as I approached near enough to distinguish the features of the old negro who led the animal, I discovered that he was a gentleman who, upon that day at least, was to be approached only with the most profound respect. His step was martial, his eye looked directly forward, and his countenance plainly indicated that he had many deep things shut up in his brain, which the world had long been trying to pry into, in vain. I concluded, however, that I might venture to ask him a question, which all who had read the morning's Chronicle could have answered. I therefore took the liberty of addressing him, as soon as he came near me, with "old man, what horse is that?" The question seemed to come like a thunder-bolt among his contemplations; and without speaking a word, he bent upon me a look which I perfectly understood to mean, "Pray, sir, where were you born and brought up?" Having been thus foiled by the old man, I resolved to try my luck with the rider; accordingly, I repeated the question to him. He stopt, and was in the act, as I thought, of answering, when the old man bawled out to him, in an angry tone—

"Come along, you Bill; never keep behind you *hoss*, when you *fuss* (first) come on the ground."

Bill obeyed promptly, and took his position by *his majesty*, who observed to him in an under tone, as he came along side—

"Never tell de name you hoss; it's bad luck."

Bill's confusion plainly showed that he ought to have known a thing so obvious, from his infancy. I was as much disconcerted as Bill; but was soon relieved by a pert little blackamoor, who, rather to persuade me that he was in all the secrets of the turf, than in charity to me, addressed me with—

"Master, I'll tell you what hoss dat is."

"Well, my boy," said I, "what horse is it?"

"He young Butteram, son o' *ole* Butteram, dat usen to belong to Mr. Swingletree."

"And do you know all the horses that are going to run to-day?" said I.

"La, yes sir;" said he: "I know ebery one dat's gwine to run ebery day."

I concluded I would take advantage of the boy's knowledge; and therefore gave him twelve and a half cents to stand by me, and give me the names of the racers as they past; for by this time they were all on the ground, and following the direction of the first.

"This one," said my Mentor, as the next approached, "name Flory Randle; she b'long to Mr. Pet; but I don't know what hoss he daddy, though."

"This one," (as the next came up) "name Sir William; he come all de way from Virginy, and I tink dey say he got by Virginy too."

"And this," (as the last approached) "name Clipse; by jokey, he look to me like he could clip it too; and I be swinged if I don't go my seb'n-pence on him any how."

Thus I learned that the four horses which were to run, were Bertrand, Flora Randolph, Sir William, and Eclipse. At this moment, a voice from the Judges' stand cried, "Prepare your horses!" and in an instant the grooms were engaged in saddling the animals. This preliminary was soon disposed of, and the owners proceeded to give the riders their instructions.

"Now, Bob," said Mr. Pet, "I know that I have the heels of any horse on the turf, but I'm a little afraid of my bottom; therefore, save your wind as much as possible. Trail the leading horse upon a hard rein, about a half distance behind, until you come to the last half mile, and then let Flora off at full speed. As soon as you pass the leading horse about a length, bear your rein, and don't come in more than a length ahead."

"Sam," said the owner of Sir William, "you've got none to fear but Bertrand, and you've got the bottom of him; therefore give him no rest from the word 'go!'—unless you find that your heels are as good as his; and if so, you need'nt waste your wind. Feel Bertrand at the first rise of the course; if he stands it pretty well, try how you can move with him, going down the hill; and if you find that you are too hard for him, either at the rises or falls, pinch him hard at all of *them* places—and when you come to the last half mile of each heat, run his heart, liver, lights, and soul-case out of him."

"Ned," said the owner of Eclipse, "you are not to run for the first heat at all, unless you find you can take it very easy. Let Sir William take the first heat.—You can beat the others when you please, and William can't stand a push for two heats; therefore, just play along side of him handsomely, for the first three miles, and at the coming in, just drop in the distance pole. The next heat take the track, and press him from the start."

"Bill," said the owner of Bertrand, "do you take the track at the start, and keep it, and run only just fast enough to keep it."

Here the roll of the drum, and a cry from the Judges' stand, put the horses in motion for the starting point. Over this point, I now observed suspended from a pole, a beautiful blue silk purse, spangled with silver, and embroidered with gold, on both sides of which were marked in golden characters, "$500"!!!

It would require a volume to describe the scene which now ensued. "Captain, do you run Bertrand for the heat?" "I do, sir." "Five hundred dollars, Bertrand against the field." "Done, sir." "Major, will Eclipse run for the heat?" "No, sir." "One hundred to fifty, that Flora Randolph beats Eclipse the first heat!" "Done, sir"—"Done, sir"— "Done, sir." "I took the bet first." "No, sir, I took it first." "No matter, gentlemen, I'll go you all fifty apiece." "It's a bet, sir"—"It's a bet"—"A bet, sir." "Here, Uncle Sam, hold dese trumps"—"Now mind de bet. Bob, he bet dat Flory Randle take de fus heat. I bet he take no heat at all." "Yes, dat de bet—you hear him, Uncle Sam?"

"Tell him over agin, le' me listen." "Well, dis him: If Flory take de fus heat, Bob win—if he take no heat at all, I win." "Berry well, I got him now fass in my head."

"Pa, give me a quarter to bet." "What horse do you want to bet upon, my son?" "Eclipse." "Oh no—there's a quarter—bet it upon Bertrand."

"Well, Miss Flora, don't you wish to bet?" "Yes, sir, I'll bet you a pair of gloves." "Well, what horse will you take?"

"Oh, my namesake, of course." "It's a bet—you take Flora against the field, of course." "To be sure I do."

Thus it went—men, women and children, whites and blacks, all betting.

Such was the bustle, confusion and uproar among the men, that I could hardly see or hear any thing distinctly; and therefore I resolved to take my position among the carriages, in order to observe the ladies under the delights of the turf.

The signal was now given, and off went the horses—Flora ahead, Bertrand next, Sir William next, and Eclipse in the rear.

"Only look at that rascal," said Mr. Pet, as he charged by us at full speed; "how he is riding. Hold her in, you rascal, or I'll give you five hundred lashes as soon as you light —Hold her in, I tell you, you abominable puppy, or I'll cut your throat." Bob did his best to restrain her, for he bore upon the rein until his back came nearly in contact with Flora's; but to no purpose.—Ahead she would go for the first two miles.

"Only see, mamma," said Miss Flora, "how beautifully Flora runs!" "Oh, that dear little rider," (*a negro,*) "how handsomely he carries himself. I knew I should win my gloves."

At the completion of the second mile, Flora became more manageable, and the other horses passed her in their order. As the last gained about a length of her—"now," said Pet, "keep her at that." The rider straightened himself in the saddle, but the space widened, perceptibly, between him and Eclipse. "Don't bear upon the rein so hard," said Pet. "Let her play easy." Bob slackened the rein; but Flora seemed not to improve her liberty. "Look how you're drop-ping behind," continued Pet. "Let her out, I tell you!" Bob *let* her out, but she would not *go out*. "Let her out, I tell you, or I will blow your brains out." Here Bob gave her a cut— "You infernal rascal you, don't give her the whip! Bring her up to Eclipse." Bob gave her the lash again; but Flora ob-stinately refused to keep company with Eclipse. "Very well, sir," said Pet, "ride your own way, and I'll whip mine when you get home; I see how it is." Bob seemed to hear only the first member of the sentence, and he gave the whip without mercy. "Why, Pet," said a gentleman, "what is the matter with Flora to-day?" "What's the matter with her, sir! Don't you see that I can't make Bob do any thing I tell him? I'll learn him how to take a *bribe* in future."

As Flora received the twentieth cut she switched her tail. "Ah!" said Mr. Dimple, "I fear you've lost your gloves Miss Flora—see, your favorite switches her tail." "Does Flora switch her tail?" said Miss Flora.—"Mamma, Mr. Dimple says Flora switches her tail?" "Does Flora switch her tail?" said Mrs. Blue. "Does Flora switch her tail?" said Miss Emma. "Oh, what a pity!"

The horses preserved their order through the heat. Flora was distanced; but her rider maintained his grace and dignity to the last, and rode as if perfectly satisfied that every eye was upon him, and that all were saying: "to be sure Flora is beaten; but her rider is decidedly the best on the ground." In spite of his cry of "clear the track!" how-ever, the crowd closed in between him and the foremost horses, extinguished his graces from general view, and forced him to come in, in the mere character of a spectator.

Between the first and second heats, I saw the owners of

Sir William and Eclipse in a pleasing conversation; but I did not hear what they said.

After a rest of about a quarter of an hour, the horses were again brought to the starting point; and at the tap of the drum went off with great velocity. Bertrand took the lead as before, and William pursued him very closely. They kept within two lengths of each other for three miles and a half, when William locked his adversary, and both riders commenced giving the whip and spur without mercy. When they came in, it was evident to my eye, that Bertrand's *rider* (for I could not see the horses' heads) was more than his width ahead of William's; but the judges decided that William won the heat by two inches and a quarter. Eclipse just saved his distance. At the close of the heat the two former exhibited a pitiable spectacle. There was not a dry hair upon either of them, and the blood streamed from the flanks and sides of both.

"Mr. Dimple," said Miss Emma, "which horse shall I bet on next time? Which seems the most distressed?"

"I declare, Miss," said Dimple, "I don't know—they both seem to be very much distressed; but I think William seems to be in rather the worse plight."

Between this and the following heat, two little boys engaged in a fight, and not less than fifty grown men gathered around them to witness the conflict, with as great an uproar as if a town were on fire. This fight produced two more between grown persons; one of whom was carried from the turf with a fractured skull, as it was thought, from the blow of a stick. But none of the ladies went to the fights.

Again the horses were brought up and put off. Bertrand once more led the way, and Eclipse followed close at his heels, for about a mile and three quarters, when William ran up under whip, nose and tail to Bertrand. Eclipse fell some distance behind, and continued so for a mile and a half, when he came up and nearly locked Bertrand. Thus they ran three fourths of the remaining distance. On the last stretch they came side to side, and so continued through. On this heat, I concurred with the judges, that it was a draw race. William was double distanced.

Bertrand and Eclipse put off upon the fourth heat: Bertrand still taking the lead by about half his length. Eclipse now pushed for the track; but Bertrand maintained it. For two miles did the riders continue so close together that they might have joined hands. They had entered upon the third mile in this way, when at the first turn of the course from the judges' stand, Eclipse fell and killed his rider. Bertrand being now left without a competitor, galloped slowly round to the goal, where with great pomp and ceremony, the pole which held the purse was bent down to his rider, who dislodged it, and bore it on high, backwards and forwards, in front of the booth, to the sound of drum, fife and violin.

"I declare," said Mrs. Blue, as her carriage wheeled off, "had it not been for that little accident, the sport would have been delightful."

I left the turf in company with a large number of gentlemen, all of whom concurred in the opinion, that they had never witnessed such sport in all their lives. "What a pity it is," said General Grubbs, "that this amusement is not more encouraged! We never shall have a fine breed of horses until the turf is more patronized."

I returned home, and had been seated perhaps an hour, when Baldwin entered. "Well," said he, "I have just been favored with a sight of the contents of that beautiful purse which Bertrand won—and what do you think it contained?"

"Why, five hundred dollars, certainly," returned I.

"No," continued he, "it contained two half eagles, sixteen dollars in silver, twelve one dollar bills, and a subscription paper, which the owner offered to the largest subscriber on it, for one hundred and fifty dollars, and it was refused. It is but right to observe, however, that the gentleman to whom the offer was made assured the owner that it was as good as gold."

HALL.

AN INTERESTING INTERVIEW.

I HOPE the day is not far distant, when drunkenness will be unknown in our highly favored country. The moral world is rising in its strength against the all-destroying vice, and though the monster still struggles, and stings, and poisons, with deadly effect, in many parts of our wide spread territory, it is perceptibly wounded and weakened; and I flatter myself, if I should live to number ten years more, I shall see it driven entirely, from the higher walks of life at least, if not from all grades of society. For the honor of my contemporaries, I would register none of its crimes or its follies; but, in noticing the peculiarities of the age in which I live, candor constrains me to give this vice a passing notice. The interview which I am about to present to my readers, exhibits it in its mildest and most harmless forms.

In the county of ———, and about five miles apart, lived old Hardy Slow and old Tobias Swift—They were both industrious, honest, sensible farmers, when sober; but they never visited their county-town, without getting drunk; and then they were—precisely what the following narrative makes them.

They both happened at the Court House on the same day, when I last saw them together; the former accompanied by his wife, and the latter by his youngest son, a lad about thirteen. Tobias was just clearly on the wrong side of the line, which divides drunk from sober; but Hardy was "*royally corned*" (but not falling) when they met, about an hour by sun in the afternoon, near the rack at which both their horses were hitched.

They stopped about four feet apart, and looked each other full in the face for about half a minute; during all which time, Toby sucked his teeth, winked, and made signs with his shoulders and elbows to the by-standers that he knew Hardy was drunk, and was going to quiz him for their amusement. In the meantime, Hardy looked at Tobias, like a polite man dropping to sleep in spite of himself, under a long dull story.

At length Toby broke silence:

"How goes it, uncle Hardy?" (*winking to the company and shrugging his shoulders.*)

"Why, Toby!—is that you? Well—upon my—why, Toby! ——Lord—help—my—soul and——Why, Toby! what, in, the, worl', set, you, to, gitt'n, drunk—this, time o' day? Swear, poin' blank, you're drunk! Why—you—must be, an

Hardy Slow and Tobias Swift

old, fool—to, get, drunk, right, before, all these, gentlemen
—a'ready, Toby."

"Well, but, now you see, (*winking*) uncle Hardy, a gill-
cup an't a quart-pot, nor a quart-pot an't a two gallon jug;
and therefore, (*winking and chuckling*) uncle Hardy, a thing
is a thing, turn it which way you will, it just sticks at what it
was before you give it first ex—ex—ploit."

"Well, the, Lord, help, my—Why, Toby! what, is the
reas'n, you, never, will, answer, me this, one—circumstance
—and, that, is—I, always, find, you, drunk, when, I come,
here."

"Well, now, but uncle Hardy, you always know circumstances alters cases, as the fellow said; and therefore, if one
circumstance alters another circumstance—how's your wife
and children?"

"I, swear, poin' blank, I shan't tell you—because, you
r'ally, is, too drunk, to know, my wife, when, you, meet,

her, in the street, all, day, long, and, she'll, tell, you, the, very, same, thing, as, all, these, gentlemen, can—testimony."

"Well, but now you see, uncle Hardy, thinking's one thing and knowing's another, as the fellow said; and the proof o' the pudding's chawin' the bag, as the fellow said; and you see—toll-doll-diddle-de-doll-doll-day, (*singing and capering*) you think I can't dance? Come, uncle Hardy, let's dance."

"Why, Toby!—you—come—to this? *I* did'nt make, you, drunk, did I? You, an't, took, a drink, with, me, this, live, long, day—is you? I, say, is you, Toby?"

"No, uncle Har—"

"Well, then, let's go, take a drink."

"Well, but you see, uncle Hardy, drinkin's drinkin'; but that's neither here nor there, as the fellow said.

"Come (*singing*) all ye young sparkers, come listen to me,
And I'll sing you a ditti, of a pretti ladee."

"Why, Toby! ha—ha—ha—Well, I r'ally, did, think, you, was, drunk, but, now I believe—blast the flies! I b'lieve, they, jest, as li'f, walk, in my, mouth, as, in, my, nose." (*Then looking with eyes half closed at Toby for several minutes,*) "Why, Toby, you, spit 'bacco spit, all over, your jacket—and, that's jist, the very, way, you, got, in your—fix."

At this moment, Mrs. Slow came up, and immediately after, Swift's son, William.

"Come," said the good lady, "old man, let's go home; it's getting late, and there's a cloud rising; we'll get wet."

"Why, Nancy! what in the worl' has got into you! Is you

drunk too? Well, 'pon, my word, and honor, I, b'lieve, every body, in this town, is, got drunk to-day. Why, Nancy! I never, did, see, you, in, that fix, before, in, all, my, live, long, born, days."

"Well, never mind," said she, "come, let's go home. Don't you see the rain coming up?"

"Well, will, it rain, upon, my, corn-field, or my cotton-patch? Say, Nancy! which one, will it, rain on? But, Lord, help, my, soul, you are, too drunk, to tell me, any, thing, about it. Don't my corn want rain, Nancy? Now, jist, tell me, that?"

"Yes; but let's go home."

"Then, why, upon, the face, of the earth, won't you, let it, rain, then? I, rather, it, should rain, than not."

"Come, old man," said several by-standers, touched with sympathy for the good lady, "come get on your horse and go home, and we will help you."

"Oh yes, uncle Hardy," said Tobias, affecting to throw all humor aside, and to become very sober all at once, "go home with the old woman—Come, gentlemen, let's help 'em on their horses—they're groggy—mighty groggy. Come, old man, I'll help you." (staggering to Hardy.)

"Jist look at daddy now!" said Billy; "he's going to help Mr. Swift, and he's drunk as Mr. Swift is. Oh, daddy, come, let's go home, or we'll get mazin' wet."

Toby stooped down to help Hardy on his horse, (before the horse was taken from the rack,) and throwing his arm round Hardy's legs, he fell backwards, and so did Hardy.

"Why—Lord, bless, my, soul," said Hardy, "I b'lieve I'm drunk too. What, upon the, face, of the earth, has got, into, all, of us, this day!"

"Why, uncle Hardy," said Toby, "you pull us both down together." "The old man's mighty groggy," said Toby to me, in a half whisper, and with an arch wink and smile, as he rose up, (I happening to be next to him at the moment,) "S'pose we help him up and get him off. The old woman's in for it too," continued he; winking, nodding, and shrugging up his shoulders very significantly.

"Oh no," said I, "the old woman is perfectly sober, and I never heard of her tasting a drop in all my life."

"Oh," said Toby, assuming the gravity of a parson, "loves it mightily, mightily!—Monstrous woman for drinking!—at least that's my opinion. Monstrous fine woman though! monstrous fine!"

"Oh, daddy, for the Lord's sake let's go home; only see what a rain is coming!" said Billy.

"Daddy'll go presently my son."

"Well here's your horse, git up and let's go. Mammy'll be sure to be sendin' for us."

"Don't mind him," said Toby, winking to me; "he's nothing but a boy; I would'nt take no notice of what he said. He wants me (*winking and smiling*) to go home with him; now you listen."

"Well, come," said I to uncle Toby, "get on your horse, and go home, a very heavy rain is coming up."

"I'll go presently, but you just listen to Bill," said he to me, winking and smiling.

"Oh, daddy, for the Lord's sake let's go home."

Toby smiled archly at me, and winked.

"Daddy, are you going home or not? Jist look at the rain comin'."

Toby smiled and winked.

"Well, I do think a drunken man is the biggest fool in the county," said Bill, "I don't care who he is."

"Bill!" said the old man, very sternly, " 'honor thy father and mother,' that—that the woman's seed may bruise the serpent's head."

"Well, daddy, tell me if you won't go home! You see it's going to rain powerful. If you won't go, may I go?"

"Bill! 'Leave not thy father who begat *thee;* for thou art my beloved son Esau, in whom I am well pleased.' "

"Why, daddy, it's dropping rain now."—Here Bill was relieved from his anxiety by the appearance of Aaron, a trusty servant, whom Mrs. Slow had despatched for his master, to whose care Bill committed him, and was soon out of sight.

Aaron's custom had long been to pick up his master without ceremony, put him on his horse, and bear him away. So used to this dealing had Toby been, that when he saw Aaron, he surrendered at discretion, and was soon on the road. But as the rain descended in torrents, before even Bill could have proceeded half a mile, the whole of them must have been drenched to the skin.

As to Hardy, whom in the proper order we ought to have disposed of first, he was put on his horse by main force; and was led off by his wife, to whom he was muttering as far as I could hear him—"Why, Nancy! How, did, you, get, in, such a fix? You'll, fall, off, your, horse, sure, as you're born, and I'll have to put you up again." As they were constrained to go in a walk, they too must have got wringing wet, though they had a quarter of an hour the start of Toby.

HALL.

THE FOX HUNT.

I HAD often read of the fox chase, and its soul-enlivening pleasures, before I was permitted to enjoy them; and had my reading upon this head been confined to Somerville's Chase alone, I should have been inspired with an irrepressible curiosity to experience its thrilling enjoyments. Listen how he sanctifies the sport, and mingles with it all that is gay and spirit-stirring:—

" But yet, alas! the wily fox remained
A subtle, pilfering foe, prowling around
In midnight shades, and wakeful to destroy.
In the full fold, the poor defenceless lamb,
Seized by his guileful arts, with sweet warm blood
Supplies a rich repast. The mournful ewe,
Her dearest treasure lost through the dim night,
Wanders perplex'd and darkling bleats in vain,
While in th' adjacent bush, poor Philomel
(Herself a parent once, till wanton churls
Despoil'd her nest,) joins in her loud laments,
With sweeter notes, and more melodious woe.
    For these nocturnal thieves, huntsmen prepare
This sharpest vengeance. Oh! how glorious 'tis
To right th' oppress'd, and bring the felon vile
To just disgrace! Ere yet the morning peep
Or stars retire from the first blush of day,
With thy far echoing voice alarm thy pack
And rouse thy bold compeers. Then to the copse
Thick with entangling grass, and prickly furze,
With silence lead thy many colour'd hounds,
In all their beauty's pride. See! how they range
Dispersed, how busily this way, and that,
They cross, examining with curious nose
Each likely haunt. Hark! on the drag I hear

Their doubtful notes, preluding to the cry
More nobly full, and swell'd with every mouth.
*   *   *   *   *
          *   *   *   *   *
Heavens! what melodious strains! how beat our hearts
Big with tumultuous joy! the loaded gales
Breathe harmony; and as the tempest drives
From wood to wood, through every dark recess,
The forest thunders and the mountains shake
*   *   *   *   *   *   *   *
*   *   *   *   *   he breaks away.
Shrill horns proclaim his flight. Each straggling hound
Strains o'er the lawn to reach the distant pack:
'Tis triumph all and joy. Now, my brave youths,
Now give a loose to the clean generous steed;
Flourish the whip nor spare the galling spur;
But in the madness of delight, forget
Your fears. For o'er the rocky hills we range
And dangerous our course; but in the brave
True courage never fails. In vain the stream
In foaming eddies whirls; in vain the ditch
Wide-gaping threatens death. The craggy steep
Where the poor dizzy shepherd crawls with care
And clings to every twig, gives us no pain;
But down we sweep, as stoops the falcon bold
To pounce his prey."   *   *   *

Filled with such ideas as these lines are calculated to inspire, (and long as is the extract, it does but half justice to the *poet,* whatever we may think of his *subject,*) it was with kindling enthusiasm that I met the question from my old friend Dause, on a clear, chill, December's evening, "Will you not join us in a fox chase to-morrow?"

"That I will," replied I, "with pleasure."

"Have you ever been in a fox chase?" continued he. "Never," said I; "but I have no doubt, but that I should be delighted with it."

"Oh, it's the finest sport in the world, with a full pack! and we shall have a splendid pack to-morrow. Major Crocket is coming in with his hounds, and George Hurt is to bring in his, and all unite with Capt. Reid's here; and we shall have a pack of twenty-two or three. We shall have glorious sport—you must not fail to join us."

"No fear of that," said I, "I shall be among the first on the ground."

I went home, (no matter where,) and hastened to bed at an earlier hour than usual, that I might be the surer to rise by times in the morning.—But, so bright was the anticipation of the coming joys, that it was long before I could compose myself to sleep; and when I did, it was rather the *semi-sleep* of vigilance, than the sound sleep of rest. It was sufficient, however, to beguile the intervening hours; and they seemed but few, before the long drawn notes of Crocket's horn roused me from my slumbers. I sprang from my bed— and without waiting to throw over me a stitch of clothing, (though the weather was extremely cold,) I seized my little ram's-horn, hoisted a window, and blew a blast, which, if it had had fair play, would have waked every hound within five miles round. But it had not fair play; for, partly from hurry, and partly from my indisposition to thrust my exposed body into the open air, I just gave the mouth of my horn projection enough to throw half its voice out and half inside the house. The first half did no great things; but the last half, did wonders. Bursting upon the unsuspecting family, at that still hour, it created a sensation which no one can understand, who was not at the falling of the walls of Jericho. The house trembled, the glasses rattled, the women started, and the children screamed.

"What's that!" exclaimed the mistress of the household.

"Mr. Hall's going a fox hunting," said her husband.

"Well, I wish he'd blow for his foxes out of the house. I can't see what any man of common sense wants to be gitting up this time of night for, in such cold weather, just to hear dogs run a fox."

It struck me, there was a good deal of sound philosophy in the good lady's remarks; but she was a *woman*, and she had never read Somerville.

I dressed myself, walked out, waked my servant and ordered my horse. Truly it was a lovely morning, for the season of the year: December never ushered in one more lovely— Like a sheet of snow, the frost overspread the earth! Not a breath was stirring—The coming huntsman had sounded his horn upon a distant hill, and its unrepeated notes had died away. A cloudless sky o'erspread the earth—as rich in beauty as ever won the gaze of mortal. Upon the western verge, in all his martial glory, stood Orion; his burnished epaulets and spangled sash, with unusual brightness glowing. Capella glittered brighter still, and Castor, Procyion and Arcturus, rivalled her in lustre. But Sirius reigned the monarch of the starry host; and countless myriads of lesser lights, glowed, and sparkled, and twinkled, o'er all the wide spread canopy. "Oh!" exclaimed I, "how rich, how beautiful, how glorious the firmament!" See! yonder is Bootes in the *chase!* His Chara and Asterion drive on the lusty Bear! who shall condemn the chase, when its pleasures are written in characters of deathless fire, upon the face of the heavens!

I was lost in admiration of the splendors which surrounded me, when another sound of the Major's horn informed me that he was upon the confines of the village; and, at the same instant, my servant announced that my horse was in waiting. As I approached him for the purpose of mounting, "Master," said my servant, "you *gwine* fox huntin' on da hose?"

"Yes," said I promptly: "why?"

"Eh-eh," rejoined he, with a titter.

"Why, what is it amuses you so, Isaac?"

"Bess de Lord! Smooth-tooth wa'nt never made for fox huntin', I know. He too lazy, bess de Lord. Time de houn' give one squall, dey done leff Smooth-tooth clean outen sight an' hearin'."

"O, I presume not, Isaac," said I. "I shall not attempt to keep up with the hounds: I shall just keep in full hearing of them by cutting across and heading them."

"Eh-eh! Fox run twice round a field 'fore Smooth-tooth cut across him, I know: bess de Lord."

One would suppose that Isaac's hint would have reminded me to take a whip or spur, or both, along with me; but it did not.

Crocket's horn was answered by several from the neighboring hills, and before I proceeded the eighth of a mile towards the point of rendezvous, a loud chorus of horns and beagles announced that all were assembled but myself. I raised my ram's horn and blew a more propitious blast than my first, in token that I was on my way. My horse, as the reader has perhaps conjectured, from the colloquy just repeated, was not Somerville's "clean, generous steed;" but he was a horse of uncommon gravity and circumspection. I gave him the name of *Smooth-tooth*, simply because when he became my property, the faces of his teeth were, generally, worn smooth. Though he was kind and accommodating enough, in all matters of business, he had an utter aversion to every thing like levity, and to all rambles which seemed to have no definite object. *Age* had done much, doubtless, in sobering Smooth-tooth's temper; but *infirmity* had conspired with age to produce this effect; for he was most lamentably deaf: so that the common remark of our State in relation to aged horses, "he has heard it thunder too often," would by no means have applied to Smooth-tooth; for to my certain knowledge he had not heard it thunder for five years at least.

I bent my course towards the village, and as Smooth-tooth was wholly unconscious of the uproar there, he set out as usual upon a gentle *pace*. By a diligent application of heels, I signified to him that I looked for something more sprightly upon this occasion. Smooth-tooth took the hint, and mended his *pace;* but I informed him as before, that this would not do.—He then paced brisker still; but this did not abate my rigor.—He then paced to the top of his speed, and finding me still unsatisfied, he struck, most reluctantly, into a lazy canter. This reduced my *beats* from *triple* to *common time*, but did not bring them to a full pause. At the end of five long, awkward, reluctant lopes, Smooth-tooth stopped with a demi-semiquaver *rest*, and wheeled at the same instant to go home, in utter disgust; for he seemed now to have satisfied himself that I had taken leave of my senses, and that it was high time for him to "throw himself upon his reserved rights." As I always entertained a high respect for these, I accommodated myself to his views, after having discovered that he was not to be *forced* out of them. There was, however, some policy mixed with my clemency; for slowly as Smooth-tooth moved in his master effort, he waked up an artificial breeze, which seemed to search the very cavities of my bones; and which already produced some unacknowledged yearnings for the comfortable bed which I had deserted.

When I reached the village, I found all the huntsmen collected; and after a little delay, occasioned by a dog fight— or rather a fight of one dog against all the rest, (for hounds, like the wiley politicians of the present day, all jump on the undermost,) we moved forward to the hunting ground. This lay three miles from the village, and could any thing have enlivened the jaunt, my company would; for it consisted of a merry group of every variety of disposition. But a freezing man cannot be lively; and consequently I was not.

Our pack consisted of eighteen or twenty hounds; but there were but two of them, which could be relied on with confidence—George Hurt's Louder, and Captain Reid's Rome. With these I was well acquainted, having often been with them in the deer and rabbit hunt. Could I say, like Horace, "*exigi monumentum ære perennius*," they should be immortalized; for better dogs never mingled in the chase. They knew perfectly well, from the hour of the hunt, and the equipments of the huntsmen, the game of which they were in pursuit; and no other would they notice.

Capt. Reid's *Music* was said to be remarkable "*cold;*" but her veracity was questionable. Her ambition never aimed at any thing higher than finding the *track*, for fleeter footed hounds. When the game was up, she soon "knocked out" and went in quest of cold trails; why, or wherefore, no one could tell—unless it was that she had the common fault of those who possess peculiar accomplishments. Her habit was, to get a trail, and if she could not lead off on it readily, to "open" by the half hour upon so much of it as lay within the compass of three rods square.

We had proceeded about two miles on our way, when, in a washed field to our right, Music opened.

"What dog's that?" inquired several voices at once.

"It's Music," said the Captain; "she's the coldest hound of the pack."

The majority were for moving on, regardless of Music's cry; but, in courtesy to the Captain, who had more confidence in her than the rest of us, we agreed "to wait on her a little."

"Speak to him, Music!" said the Captain.

Music opened again.

"Try for him, Music."

Music opened again.

"Let's go to her," said the Captain; "there's not much confidence to be placed in her, but it may be a fox."

We went, and as soon as Music saw us she seemed highly delighted at our attentions—ran into a little gully—put her nose to the ground—seemed in doubt—rooted in the dirt a little way—then raised her head—paused a second, and trotted round a circle of ten yards circumference, opening all the time as if the whole horizon was lined with foxes—that is, as though there were an abundance of foxes about, but they were a long way off.

"Try for him again, Music!" said the Captain. Music fidgetted about with great animation, shook her tail spiritedly, and after taking a sweep of sixty feet, returned to the gully, and did as before.

"I'm afraid it's too cold," said the Captain.

"Oh, no," said Colonel Peyton waggishly; "let's wait on

her. 'Bundance o' foxes in that gully—only give Music time, and she'll fill it full o' dead foxes before sunrise."

"I reckon," said Stewart Andrews, in a long drawling dry way, "that Music has got upon a 'Miss Mary Ann' that went along there last winter."

The reader must here be informed, that when I went into the neighborhood of which I have been speaking, the common appellation of the rabbit, was "Molly Cotton-tail," as it still is, elsewhere in Georgia; but, as I thought this inelegant, if not vulgar, I prevailed upon my fellow-huntsmen to exchange it for a more classic term, which would preserve the sense, without offending the most squeamish delicacy. At my suggestion, therefore, it was called the "Mary Cotton-tail," and afterwards, by further refinement, "Miss Mary Ann Cotton-tail."—But to return:

We were just about taking leave of Music, when a young, awkward, overgrown hound, trotted up to her assistance. He arrived just as Music had paid a third visit to the track in the gully, and as soon as she left it, he put his nose to the spot, snuffed a little, and then raised one foot, and with it kindly scratched out the tantalizing track. While I sat "waiting upon" Miss Music, my freezing limbs forced me into this train of reflection: "How could I have so far taken leave of my senses, as to promise myself any pleasure from such a jaunt as this!—It is extremely doubtful whether we shall start a fox; and if we should, what are the cries of twenty hounds, to three or four hours exposure, without even an overcoat, upon such a piercing morning as this! And wherein will the cry differ from that of the same pack, in pursuit of a rabbit, on a fine sunny day. And why seek amusement in the tortures of a poor unoffending animal! In this country, at least, I never heard of a single loss from a farm-yard which could be fairly traced to the fox—not even of a goose, much less of a lamb. My rest broken, my health jeoparded, and my immediate sufferings excrutiating! Folly—madness in the extreme!"

We had not proceeded far before groups of from two to five hounds could be heard in all directions in pursuit of *Miss Mary Anns*. Hitherto my hopes had been buoyed up, by the *number* of hounds; for I naturally concluded, that our chances of success increased with their number: but now, I plainly saw that our only hope was upon Rome and Louder, for all the others had resigned themselves unreservedly to Mary Anns.

We were moving on upon a skirt of woods, entirely surrounded by fields, when from the opposite side of it, the well known voice of the deep-mouthed Louder fell joyously upon our ears. "Hark!" cried all of us at once. In an instant, the clear, shrill note of Rome confirmed his companion's report; for they always hunted together, and each obeyed the call of the other in a moment. Then both together—then alternately in quick succession, they repeated their assurances. In an instant all the various groups of hounds of which we were speaking, were hushed; and from every direction they could be seen dashing to the two favorites. Such is the force of truth even with dumb brutes.

A loud scream of exultation and encouragement broke involuntarily from all the huntsmen, (not excepting myself,) and each dashed for the hounds as the impulse of the moment urged him on. Some skirted the forest in one way, some in another; but Crocket plunged directly through it at half speed—how, heaven only knows; but I hardly missed him before I heard him encouraging the dogs in his presence. I took a moment for reflection, which, of course, I was permitted to enjoy alone. My conclusion was, that if Crocket could *gallop* through the wood with safety, I certainly could *pace* through it without injury, and as this was much the nearest way, I determined to attempt it. My resolves were no sooner formed than they were communicated to Smooth-tooth, who entered the wood with his accustomed prudence and circumspection.

The first streaks of day had now appeared; but they were entirely useless to me after I entered the forest. I had proceeded about sixty paces, when a limb, of some kind, (I know not what,) fetched me a whipe across the face, that set the principles of philosophy at defiance; for it was certainly four times as severe, as Smooth-tooth's momentum would have justified, upon any known law of projectiles— At least it seemed so to me; for it came like a flash of lightning over the icing of my face; giving me, for the first time in my life, a *sensible* idea of the Georgia expression, "feeling streaked;" for my face actually felt as though it was covered with streaks of fire and streaks of ice.

Twenty paces more, had like to have wound up my hunt with the felon's death: for, as I was moving on with all due caution and sobriety, a little, supple, infrangible grape vine, attached to two slim elastic sapplings, between which I passed, threw one of its festoons gracefully around my neck, and politely informed me that I must stop, or be hung. I communicated this intelligence to Smooth-tooth without loss of time, and as *stopping* was his delight, he, of course, obeyed the mandate as quick as he could. Prompt as was his obedience, it was too slow for the petulant little grape vine;

The Fox-Hunt

for, though it consented to spare my life, it dismissed me with most ungentlemanly rudeness. It just took my profile from my neck upwards, passing over all the turns and angles of my face, with a rigor that Socrates himself could not have borne with patience. It returned from its delineation, like a bow-string, sending my hat aloft, I know not how high; but judging from the time which intervened between its departure from my head, and its report on the ground, I should say nearly to the height of the wedded sapplings. Never but once before, had I such a lively sense of the value of a hat in cold weather, as I now had. The chills ran from my head to my toes, like ague fits; and these I had to bear for the space of a minute or two, before I could *feel out* my hat. At last I recovered it and remounted. "How was it possible," exclaimed I, "for Crocket to get through this wood at half speed! It must be true, that '*fortuna favet fortibus*,' and I'll e'en risk a little upon the strength of the maxim. *Swit-*

ches were convenient, as my misfortunes have proved; and having supplied myself with one, I drew my hat over my eyes, brought my head down close to Smooth-tooth's withers, hugged him tight with my legs, and put whip to him manfully. Smooth-tooth now felt his *dignity* assailed, and he put off at a respectable fox hunting gait. This soon brought me to the edge of the old field, with no other accident than a smart blow from a sappling, upon my right knee, which, though it nearly unhorsed me, did me no serious injury.

Here I found all my companions re-assembled.—While the drag lay within the frost-covered field, the dogs carried it briskly; but as soon as it entered the wood, they were at fault. In this situation they were, when I joined the huntsmen. It was long before we had any encouragement to hope that they would ever take it beyond the margin of the field; occasionally, however, and at painful intervals, the two favorites would bid us not to despair. Crocket, and three or four of the party, remained with and encouraged the hounds; while Andrews, Marden and myself, adjourned to a narrow lane to enjoy the comforts of the risen sun. The sluggish trail allowed us an hour's basking; which so far relaxed my rigid members as to prepare me for enjoying Marden's amusing stories, and Stewart's dry humor. While we were thus engaged, and after we had relinquished all hope of a chase for that morning at least, the notes of the two favorites became more and more frequent. Soon a third, and fourth voice joined them, and the chorus swelled and varied with every second, until eight in the morning, when the whole pack broke in full cry. Reynard was up, and twenty foes in hot pursuit.

How, or why, I am unable to tell, but truth constrains me

to say, that for some moments I was enraptured with the sport. The fox obliqued towards us, and entered a field of which our position commanded a full view. He must have left his covert with reluctance, for he was not more than a hundred paces ahead of the hounds when he entered the field. First of the pack, and side by side, the heroes of the clamorous band, rose the fence.—Then followed, in thick array, the whole troop; and close on their rear, Crocket burst through the copse-wood and charged the fence, without a pause. Around me, in every direction, I could see the huntsmen sweeping to the choir; and as emerging from the forests, or gaining the heights around, they caught the first glimpse of the gallant pack, they raised a shout, which, none but the overcharged heart can give, and none but the lifeless heart receive unmoved. I was soon deserted as before; but partly from the inspiration of the sport, and partly from the success of my recent experiment, I plied Smooth-tooth with the whip most *astonishingly*, and put off in pursuit of the hounds in handsome style—via the lane, which happened to have exactly the curvature which I desired.

The fox had hardly left the field through which my eye followed him, before all of a sudden, the voice of every hound hushed. They were completely at fault; and thus I found them when I once more joined my company. They "knocked out," as the saying is, near to the corner of 'Squire Snibby's field, which lay contiguous to the first which they entered. Dogs and men here toiled assiduously to take the trail away, but in vain. At length Crocket suspected Reynard of a trick: he conjectured that the cunning rogue had ascended the Squire's fence, and followed it some distance before he alighted. And so it proved to be; for, taking some

of the dogs with him along the fence side, Crocket introduced them again to the trail, at the distance of full three
hundred yards from the point at which they lost it.—The
cry was now renewed with all its former spirit. The fox,
huntsmen and hounds, took to the right; but as fields lay in
that direction, I concluded that he would soon turn and follow the belt of woodland, in the opposite direction; I therefore took to the left, by a pretty little path, which might possibly have exerted some influence upon my determination.
I had not proceeded far before I encountered a large log lying directly across my path. Here I resolved to experiment a
little, unobserved, upon Smooth-tooth's agility. "If," said I,
"he clears that log, in handsome style, I'll charge the first
(low) fence that intercepts my pursuit." Accordingly, I put
whip and heels to Smooth-tooth, who neared it elegantly;
but as soon as he came within jumping distance, he stopt
with a suddenness and self-composure, which plainly signified that he expected me to let it down for him. The consequence was, that I was very near being laid across the log
for my pains. I now became testy, and resolved, that as he
would not "run and jump" it, he should "stand and jump"
it. I therefore brought him up to it, and commenced the old
discipline. After proposing to go round it, either way, without my approbation, he at length raised his fore-feet, and
threw them lazily over the log, coming down upon them as
the white bear does in breaking ice, and stopt right astride
of the log. I was now prompted by curiosity to see, if left to
himself, whether he would stand there or go on; and strange
as it may seem, his own free will led him to neither alternative—for he was in the very act of drawing his fore-feet
back, with a kind of *fall-down* motion, when I gave him the

whip and forced him to drag, rather lift, his hind feet over.

This feat performed, I moved on about two hundred yards, when, as I had anticipated, I heard the hounds coming directly towards me. I stopt, and in a minute's time, Reynard crossed the path within thirty steps of me. Then came the dogs in the order in which they entered the field; and hard upon them came Crocket upon his foaming steed.

"Did you see him?" exclaimed he, finding me near the trail.

"Yes," said I, "distinctly."

"How was his tail?"

"I did'nt notice, particularly, but sticking to him I believe."

"Oh, nonsense!" said Crocket; "was his brush up or down?"

"Neither," said I, "he *brushed* right across."

Here the Major uttered something harsh and dashed on. I afterwards learned that experienced fox hunters know the extent of his exhaustion, from the manner in which he carries his tail.

Having *reasoned* out the fox's movement this time successfully, I concluded I could do the like again: I therefore reasoned, that after rambling about a short time, he would seek the neighborhood of his burrow. Accordingly I paced back (going around the log this time) to a position where I might intercept him. Here I remained about an hour, without hearing man, horse, or dog: and then I paced home, where I arrived at eleven o'clock, perfectly satisfied with fox hunting.

When my companions returned, they reported, that five miles from where I was waiting for the fox, and seven from the village, at about two o'clock, P.M., right in the big road, near Richland Creek, the dogs "knocked out," and could never be *knocked in* again.

But they brought home a rich fund of anecdote from the chase, which served to enliven many an idle hour afterwards—I reserved mine to the present moment, to enliven the family fire-side, on these cold winter's evenings.

HALL.

THE WAX WORKS.

IN the city of ———, resided once, a band of gay spirits, who, though they differed from each other in some respects, were all alike in this, that they were fond of fun.

Billy Grossly was an odd compound of grave and humorous. He seldom projected a scheme of amusement; but never failed to take part in it, when it was set on foot by others. Why, it was not easy to tell; for, if he enjoyed the most amusing pastime at all, his enjoyment was all inward; for he rarely laughed, or gave any other visible sign of lively pleasure.

Jack Clomes seemed to have been made for fun. It was his meat and his drink: he could no more live without it, than he could live without his ordinary diet. Withal, Jack had a wonderful talent for manufacturing food for his prevailing appetite. Indeed, his fault was, that he never could be got to perform his part, in a humorous exhibition, which required concert with others, without digressing from the main plot, whenever he discovered a fair opportunity of picking up a delicate morsel of fun, precisely suited to his own palate.

James McLass, was fond of a harmless frolic, and whenever he engaged in it, if by preconcert, he always made it a point of honor to perform his part in strict obedience to the original design.

These three, with six or eight others, whose dispositions it is not necessary to mention, visited the village of ———, in order to attend the races, which were in progress in the vicinity of that place.

Towards the close of the races, it was discovered that the joint funds of the whole fraternity, were not sufficient to discharge the tavern bills of any two of them. What was to be done in this emergency. To have borrowed would have been extremely mortifying, and perhaps a little inconvenient—to have gone away without paying their tavern bills, would have been contrary to the first principles of Georgia honor. They were soon relieved from their dilemma, by the ingenuity of Clomes.

During the races, a "Down-easter" had been exhibiting wax figures in the village; and concluding that the profits of his business would end with the sports of the turf, he had begun to pack up his portables, for removal to a more eligible station.

Clomes now proposed, that his company should take the places and parts of the retiring figures—or, to use his own expression—"should play wax works," until they made enough to pay their bills. A single night, it was thought, would suffice for this purpose.

The plan was no sooner proposed, than it was embraced by all. The room and its furniture were engaged for the evening; the parts were cast without difficulty; and each went industriously to work, to fit himself for the part he was to perform.

Billy Grossly, having the advantage of all the rest, in height and abdominal rotundity, was by common consent chosen as a proper representative of Daniel Lambert; the prodigious Englishman, who weighed, if I remember rightly, upwards of six hundred pounds. The reader need hardly be told, that with all his advantages, Billy required the aid of at least eight pillows, with some extra *chinking*, as we say in Georgia, to give him a bulk corresponding with this enormous weight: nor need he be told, that divers of the most decent bags which the village afforded, with a small sheet, were put in requisition, to contain him and his adjuncts.

Freedom Lazenby, was the only one of the company who could, with any propriety, personify the Sleeping Beauty; and of course this part was assigned to him. Freedom's figure was quite too gross for the beau ideal of female symmetry; and his face, though fine for a man, had rather too much compass to represent nature's finest touches of female beauty. However, it was soon perceived that a counterpane would hide the defects of the first, and a deep-frilled cap would reduce the last to passable effeminacy. But there were two other difficulties, which were not so easily removed. It is well known, that the interest of the Sleeping Beauty is much enlivened by an exposed bosom, by which reposes a lovely infant. Even Clomes' ingenuity could not

supply these. A *living* child would not answer; for whether
taken to the arms of the Beauty asleep or awake, it would be
certain to give signs of life, before the exhibition ended; and
there was not even a tolerable manufacturer of bosoms in
the whole village. There was no alternative; the interest of
the spectators must yield to the necessities of the performers:
it was therefore determined that the Beauty's bosom should
share the fate of her person, and be covered; that an infant
should be manufactured in the best possible style, out of
rags; and that the paint-brush should supply the place of
wax, for the face. As there were no Raphaels, Titians, Wests
or Debuffes, in the village, the little innocent did not come
from the hands of the artist, with the most perfect face imaginable; but it was the best that could be given to it, and if it
wanted interest, that was not the fault of the company.

To James McLass was assigned the part of Miss Eliza
Failes, the unfortunate girl who was murdered by her unnatural lover, Jason Fairbanks; and Clomes took the part of
the murderer.

It was proposed to represent Miss Failes at that moment
when the blood was streaming from the lacerated throat;
but Jemmy refused to personify her in that condition, and
therefore they had to place him in another part of the trag-
edy. That was selected, in which Fairbanks has his victim
by the hair with the left hand, the knife upraised in the
right, in the act of commencing his work of butchery.

The other figures, being merely distinguished personages,
were easily represented.

From some cause unknown, perhaps to invite visitors, or
merely because, perhaps, it was a matter that lay fully within the range of the company's art, they resolved to exhibit a

corpse in the ante-chamber, gratis; and Pleasant Halgroce, a jolly son of Bacchus, kindly offered to play this part. Every child knows, that a plate of burning spirits, with a little salt thrown into it, will throw over the features of a living person, all the paleness and ghastliness of death. This was the only device used, to convert Pleasant's smerky red face into that of a corpse.

All matters being now arranged, and the performers having practised their parts in their new characters until they ceased to be ridiculous; they all took their places after an early supper.

Before the doors were opened to the principal exhibition, a little incident occurred in the ante-chamber, which suddenly closed the entertainment in this quarter; and had a material bearing upon that in the other.

Pleasant Halgroce had taken his position, and was playing a corpse to the life, or rather to the *death*, a number of persons gathered round him, with becoming solemnity, when a dumb man, who was devotedly attached to him joined the group. As soon as his eyes fell upon the prostrate body of Pleasant, he burst into the most piteous and unaffected wailing. Nothing could restrain him from embracing his departed friend. He approached him, and was in the act of bending over him, to give him affection's fondest adieu, when a pretty stiff breeze from Pleasant's lips, strengthened by previous suppression, charged with the fumes of about a half pint of brandy, saluted the face of the mourner. The transition from grief to joy was instantaneous with the poor mute. He rose in transports—pointed to Pleasant's face, then to his own, touched his nose, gave it a significant curl, snuffed gently, and then clapping both hands to his stomach, he commenced inhaling and respiring, with all the tone and emphasis of a pair of blacksmith's bellows. Pleasant, now perceiving that exposure was inevitable, rose, and rushed upon the dumb man, with the fury of a tiger. This sudden resuscitation of Pleasant, to life in its most healthful action, was as alarming to the mute, as his breathing had been joyous; and he fled, with Pleasant at his heels, as though all the tenants of the church yard had risen upon him at once.

Pleasant had only to resume his dress, and appear in a natural light, to pass unknown by all but the initiated; for aside from burning brandy, he was no more like a corpse than a rose is like a lily.

Pleasant being now out of employment, determined to take upon himself the part of historian to the wax figures.

The door leading to the figures was no sooner opened, than several persons entered, and viewed them with apparent satisfaction. The spectators had increased to the

The Waxworks

number of eight or ten, when a raw-boned, awkward, gawky son of the forest, named Rory Brushwood, made his appearance, paid his money, and entered. Pleasant, of course, undertook to enrich his mind with historic lore, while he feasted his eye upon the wonders of art.

"This," said Pleasant, leading Rory up to the Sleeping Beauty, "is the Sleeping Beauty: she's given up on all hands to be the prettiest creature in the universal world. Now, what would you give, my old Snort, to have as pretty a wife and as pretty a baby as that?"

"Humph," said Rory, "I don't think she's so d——n'd pretty as she mout be: and as for the baby, it looks like a screech-owl in petticoats."

"Monstrous pretty, monstrous pretty!" continued Pleasant. "But come here"—hurrying Rory off, lest his remarks should wake the Sleeping Beauty—"come here, and I'll show you something that'll make your hair rise like a fighting cat's."

"There!" continued he, pointing to Billy Grossly, "just take a squint at that fellow, will you: That's Daniel Lambert: he was born in Nocatchey, and was raised upon nothing but grass-nuts and sweet potatoes; and just see what he's come to! He weighs nine hundred and fifty, dead weight."

"He's a whaler!" said Rory; "but his face is mighty little, for his belly and legs."

"Oh," said Pleasant, "that's owing to the grass-nuts and potatoes: you know they always puff up the lower parts, mightily."

Nobody but Billy could have withstood this lecture upon himself, without a smile; but he passed it off admirably.

The critical time was now at hand. Pleasant and Rory

advanced in front of Miss Failes and Mr. Fairbanks, where they found another visitor viewing the interesting couple. Pleasant deemed it unadvisable to continue his lectures in the presence of Clomes; and had Clomes himself been equally prudent, things might all have ended well: but he was not.

While the three gentlemen just named were gazing on the figures before them, Jack took it into his head to try a little experiment upon Miss Failes' muscles, through the sensibilities of her head; accordingly he tightened his grip suddenly upon her hair. This brought from her a slight wince; but Jack did not perceive it. Encouraged by her philosophy, he made a second pull with all the strength that lay in the muscles and sinews of his left hand.

This brought a palpable grin from Miss Failes; and, what was worse, in the zeal of his experiments upon Jim's stoicism, Jack over-acted his own part a little.

"Gentlemen," said Rory, in a tone of awful dignity and self-satisfaction, as he turned gravely to the bystanders, "gentlemen, it's flesh and blood."

"There," said Pleasant, "that just proves what I've said: that these are the best wax works that ever was showed in all these parts. It's most impossible to tell 'em from live folks."

"Gentlemen," repeated Rory; with the same unruffled composure, "it's flesh and blood. If I did'nt see that fellow wink, and that woman *squinch* her face, then hell's a dancing room."

"No matter for that," said Pleasant, "they're nothin' but wax for all that: and if you don't b'lieve me, just feel that fellow's cheek."

Rory raised his finger slowly, as if actually doubting the evidence of his senses, and was just in the act of touching Jack's cheek, when Jack snapped at his finger like a shark, and caught it between his teeth with a force most unreasonable for fun.

The shock was so unexpected and severe, that it completely unmanned Rory for the instant, and he sunk powerless upon the floor. He soon rose, however, and rose with Miss Failes' chair, which happened to be vacant just at this moment; and then, (to use an expression of one of the characters,) "if ever you saw wax works cut dirt, they cut it then."

Mr. Fairbanks was the first to make his escape; but not without being nearly overtaken by the chair. Miss Failes followed next—then General Washington and other distinguished personages, whose attitudes prepared them for running. The Sleeping Beauty being a little incumbered with bed-clothes, was rather slow in retiring; she was enough in a hurry, however, to leave her little infant in the middle of the floor, to Rory's care; who, discovering its true character just as Daniel Lambert was removing his feathers to another apartment, let him have the baby, with all his force, between the shoulders. As this was only rags against pillows, Daniel escaped as free from injury as the rest of them.

Rory now became clamorous for his money; but the door-keeper was not to be found; and indeed claimed, and kept, for his services, all that was made; leaving the performers to settle their bills as they could.

HALL.

A SAGE CONVERSATION.

I LOVE the aged matrons of our land. As a class, they are the most pious, the most benevolent, the most useful, and the most harmless of the human family. Their life, is a life of good offices. At home, they are patterns of industry, care, economy and hospitality; abroad, they are ministers of comfort, peace and consolation. Where affliction is, there are they, to mitigate its pangs; where sorrow is, there are they to assuage its pains. Nor night, nor day, nor summer's heat, nor winter's cold, nor angry elements, can deter them from scenes of suffering and distress. They are the first at the fevered couch, and the last to leave it. They hold the first and last cup to the parched lip. They bind the aching head, close the dying eye, and linger in the death-stricken habitation, to pour the last drop of consolation into the afflicted bosoms of the bereaved. I cannot, therefore, ridicule them myself, nor bear to hear them ridiculed in my presence. And yet, I am often amused at their conversations; and have amused *them* with a rehearsal of their own conversations, taken down by me when they little dreamed that I was listening to them. Perhaps my reverence for their character, conspiring with a native propensity to extract amusement from all that passes under my observation, has accustomed me to pay a uniformly strict attention to all they say in my presence.

This much in extraordinary courtesy to those who cannot distinguish between a simple narrative of an amusing interview, and ridicule of the parties to it. Indeed I do not know that the conversation which I am about to record, will be considered amusing by any of my readers. Certainly the amusement of the readers of my own times, is not the leading object of it, or of any of the "Georgia Scenes;" forlorn as may be the hope, that their main object will ever be answered.

When I seated myself to the sheet now before me, my intention was merely to detail a conversation between three ladies, which I heard many years since; confining myself to only so much of it, as sprung from the ladies' own thoughts, unawaked by the suggestions of others; but, as the manner of its introduction will perhaps interest some of my readers, I will give it.

I was travelling with my old friend, Ned Brace, when we stopped at the dusk of the evening at a house on the road side, for the night. Here we found three nice, tidy, aged matrons, the youngest of whom could not have been under sixty; one of them of course was the lady of the house, whose husband, old as he was, had gone from home upon a land exploring expedition. She received us hospitably, had our horses well attended to, and soon prepared for us a comfortable supper. While these things were doing, Ned and I engaged the other two in conversation; in the course of which, Ned deported himself with becoming seriousness. The kind lady of the house occasionally joined us, and became permanently one of the party, from the time the first dish was placed on the table. At the usual hour, we were summoned to supper; and as soon as we were seated, Ned, unsolicited, and most unexpectedly to me, said grace.—I knew full well that this was a prelude to some trick, I could not conjecture what. His explanation (except so much as I discovered myself) was, that he knew that one of us would

be asked to say grace, and he thought he might as well save
the good ladies the trouble of asking. The matter was, however, more fully explained just before the moment of our retiring to bed arrived. To this moment the conversation went
round between the good ladies and ourselves, with mutual
interest to all.—It was much enlivened by Ned, who was
capable, as the reader has been heretofore informed, of
making himself extremely agreeable in all company; and
who, upon this occasion, was upon his very best behaviour.
It was immediately after I had looked at my watch in token
of my disposition to retire for the night, that the conversation turned upon marriages, happy and unhappy, strange,
unequal, runaways, &c. Ned rose in the midst of it, and
asked the landlady where we should sleep. She pointed to
an open shed-room adjoining the room in which we were
sitting, and separated from it by a log partition, between
the spaces of which might be seen all that passed in the dining
room; and so close to the fireplace of this apartment, that
a loud whisper might be easily heard from one to the other.

"The strangest match," said Ned, resuming the conversation with a parson's gravity, "that ever I heard of, was that
of George Scott and David Snow; two most excellent men,
who became so much attached to each other that they actually got married"—

"The lackaday!" exclaimed one of the ladies.

"And was it really a fact?" enquired another.

"Oh yes, ma'am," continued Ned, "I knew them very
well, and often went to their house; and no people could
have lived happier or managed better than they did. And
they raised a lovely parcel of children—as fine a set as I ever
saw, except their youngest son, Billy: he was a little wild,

but, upon the whole, a right clever boy himself.—Come, friend Baldwin, we're setting up too late for travellers." So saying, Ned moved to the shed-room and I followed him.

The ladies were left in silent amazement; and Ned, suspecting, doubtless, that they were listening for a laugh from our chamber, as we entered it, continued the subject with unabated gravity, thus: "You knew those two men, did'nt you?"

"Where did they live?" enquired I, not a little disposed to humor him.

"Why, they lived down there, on Cedar Creek, close by Jacob Denman's—Oh, I'll tell you who their daughter Nancy married—She married John Clarke—you knew *him* very well."

"Oh, yes," said I, "I knew John Clarke very well.—*His* wife *was* a most excellent woman."

"Well, the boys were just as clever, for boys, as she was, for a girl, except Bill; and I never heard any thing *very* bad of him; unless it was his laughing in church; that put me more out of conceit of him than any thing I ever knew of him—Now, Baldwin, when I go to bed, I go to bed *to sleep*, and not to talk; and, therefore, from the time my head touches the pillow, there must be no more talking. Besides, we must take an early start to-morrow, and I'm tired." So saying, he hopped into his bed; and I obeyed his injunctions.

Before I followed his example, I could not resist the temptation of casting an eye through the cracks of the partition to see the effect of Ned's wonderful story upon the kind ladies. Mrs. Barney (it is time to give their names) was setting in a thoughtful posture; her left hand supporting her

chin, and her knee supporting her left elbow. Her countenance was that of one who suffers from a slight tooth-ache.
Mrs. Shad leaned forward, resting her fore-arm on her
knees, and looking into the fire as if she saw *groups of children*
playing in it. Mrs. Reed, the landlady, who was the fattest
of the three, was thinking and laughing alternately at short
intervals. From my bed, it required but a slight change of
position to see any one of the group at pleasure.

I was no sooner composed on my pillow, than the old
ladies drew their chairs close together, and began the following colloquy in a low undertone, which rose as it progressed:

Mrs. Barney. Did'nt that man say them was two *men* that
got married to one another?

Mrs. Shad. It seemed to me so.

Mrs. Reed. Why to be sure he did.—I know he said so; for
he said what their names was.

Mrs. B. Well, in the name o' sense, what did the man
mean by saying they raised a fine pa'cel o' children?

Mrs. R. Why, bless your heart and soul, honey! that's
what I've been thinkin' about. It seems mighty curious to
me some how or other. I can't study it out, no how.

Mrs. S. The man must be jokin', certainly.

Mrs. R. No, he was'nt jokin'; for I looked at him, and he
was just as much in yearnest as any body I ever *seed;* and besides, no *Christian* man would tell such a story in that solemn
way. And did'nt you hear that other man say he knew their
da'ter Nancy?

Mrs. S. But la' messy! Mis' Reed, it can't be so. It does'nt
stand to reason, don't you know it don't?

Mrs. R. Well, I would'nt think so; but it's hard for me,
some how, to dispute a *Christian* man's word.

Mrs. B. I've been thinking the thing all over in my mind, and I reckon—now I don't say it is so, for I don't know nothing at all about it—but I reckon that one o' them men was a woman dress'd in men's clothes; for I've often hearn o' women doin' them things, and following their True-love to the wars, and bein' a watin'-boy to 'em and all sich.

Mrs. S. Well, may be it's some how in that way—but la' me! 'twould o' been obliged to been found out; don't you know it would? Only think how many children she had. Now it stands to reason, that at some time or other it must have been found out.

Mrs. R. Well, I'm an old woman any how, and I reckon the good man won't mind what an old woman says to him; so bless the Lord, if I live to see the morning, I'll ask him about it.

I knew that Ned was surpassed by no man living in extricating himself from difficulties; but how he was to escape from this, with even tolerable credit to himself, I could not devise.

The ladies here took leave of Ned's marvellous story, drew themselves closely round the fire, lighted their pipes, and proceeded as follows:

Mrs. B. Jist before me and my old man was married, there was a gal name Nancy Mountcastle, (puff—puff,) and she was a mighty likely gal—(puff) I know'd her mighty well—she dressed herself up in men's clothes— (puff, puff,) and followed Jemmy Darden from P'ankatank, in KING AND QUEEN—(puff) clean up to LOUDON.

Mrs. S. (puff, puff, puff, puff, puff.) And did he marry her?

Mrs. B. (sighing deeply.) No: Jemmy did'nt marry her— pity he had'nt, poor thing.

Mrs. R. Well, I know'd a gal on Tar river, done the same thing—(puff, puff, puff.) She followed Moses Rusher 'way down somewhere in the South State—(puff, puff.)

Mrs. S. (puff, puff, puff, puff.) And what did he do?

Mrs. R. Ah—(puff, puff,) Lord bless your soul, honey, I can't tell you what he did. Bad enough.

Mrs. B. Well, now it seems to me—I don't know much about it—but it seems to me men don't like to marry gals that take on that way. It looks like it puts 'em out o' concait of 'em.

Mrs. S. I know'd one man that married a woman that followed him from Car'lina to this State; but she did'nt dress herself in men's clothes. You both know 'em.—You know Simpson Trotty's sister and Rachæl's son, Reuben. 'Twas him and his wife.

Mrs R. and Mrs. B. Oh, yes, I know 'em mighty well.

Mrs. S. Well, it was his wife—she followed him out to this State.

Mrs. B. I know'd 'em all mighty well. Her da'ter Lucy was the littlest teeny bit of a thing when it was born I ever did see. But they tell me that when I was born—now I don't know any thing about it myself—but the old folks used to tell me, that when I was born, they put me in a quart-mug, and mought o' covered me up in it.

Mrs. S. The lackaday!

Mrs. R. What ailment did Lucy die of, Mis 'Barney?

Mrs. B. Why, first she took the ager and fever, and took a 'bundance o' doctor's means for that. And then she got a powerful bad cough, and it kept gittin' worse and worse, till at last it turned into a consumption, and she jist nat'ly wasted away, till she was nothing but skin and bone, and she died; but, poor creater, she died mighty happy; and I think in my heart, she made the prettiest corpse, considerin', of any body I most ever seed.

Mrs. R. and Mrs. S. Emph! (solemnly.)

Mrs. R. What did the doctors give her for the fever and ager?

Mrs. B. Oh, they gin' her a 'bundance o' truck—I don't know what all; and none of 'em holp her at all. But at last she got over it, some how or other. If they'd have just gin' her a sweat o' bitter yerbs, jist as the spell was comin' on, it would have cured her right away.

Mrs. R. Well, I reckon sheep-saffron the onliest thing in nater for the ager.

Mrs. B. I've always hearn it was wonderful in hives, and measly ailments.

Mrs. R. Well, it's jist as good for an ager—it's a powerful sweat. Mrs. Clarkson told me, that her cousin Betsey's aunt Sally's Nancy was cured sound and well by it, of a hard shakin' ager.

Mrs. S. Why you don't tell me so!

Mrs. R. Oh bess your heart, honey, it's every word true; for she told me so with her own mouth.

Mrs. S. "A hard, hard shakin' ager!!"

Mrs. R. Oh yes, honey, it's the truth.

Mrs. S. Well, I'm told that if you'll wrap the inside skin of an egg round your little finger, and go three days reg'lar to a young persimmon, and tie a string round it, and every day, tie three knots in it, and then not go agin for three days, that the ager will leave you.

Mrs. B. I've often hearn o' that, but I don't know about it. Some people don't believe in it.

Mrs. S. Well, Davy Cooper's wife told me, she did'nt believe in it; but she tried it, and it cured her sound and well.

Mrs. R. I've hearn of many folks bein' cured in that way. And what did they do for Lucy's cough, Mis' Barney?

Mrs. B. Oh dear me, they gin' her a powerful chance o' truck. I reckon, first and last, she took at least a pint o' lodimy.

Mrs. S. and Mrs. R. The law!

Mrs. S. Why that ought to have killed her, if nothing else. If they'd jist gin' her a little cumfry and alecampane, stewed in honey, or sugar, or molasses, with a little lump o' mutton suet or butter in it: it would have cured her in two days sound and well.

Mrs. B. I've always counted cumfry and alecampane the lead of all yerbs for colds.

Mrs. S. Horehound and sugar 's mazin good.

Mrs. B. Mighty good—mighty good.

Mrs. R. Powerful good. I take mightily to a sweat of sage-tea, in desperate bad colds.

Mrs. S. And so do I, Mis' Reed. Indeed I have a great leanin' to sweats of yerbs, in all ailments sich as colds, and rheumaty pains, and pleurisies, and sich—they're wonderful good. Old brother Smith came to my house from Bethany meeting, in a mighty bad way, with a cold, and cough, and his throat and nose all stopt up; seemed like it would 'most take his breath away, and it was dead o' winter, and I had nothin' but dried yerbs, sich as camomile, sage, pennyroyal, catmint, horehound, and sich; so I put a hot rock to his feet, and made him a large bowl o' catmint tea, and I reckon he drank most two quarts of it through the night, and it put him in a mighty fine sweat, and loosened all the *phleem,* and opened all his head; and the next morning, says he to me, says he, sister Shad—you know he's a mighty kind spoken man, and always was so 'fore he joined society; and the old man likes a joke yet right well, the old man does; but he's a mighty good man, and I think he prays with greater libity, than most any one of his age I most ever seed —Don't you think he does, Mis' Reed?

Mrs. R. Powerful.

Mrs. B. Who did he marry?

Mrs. S. Why, he married—stop, I'll tell you directly— Why, what does make my old head forget so?

Mrs. B. Well, it seems to me I don't remember like I used to. Did'nt he marry a Ramsbottom?

Mrs. R. No. Stay, I'll tell you who he married presently —Oh, stay! why I'll tell you who he married!—He married old daddy Johny Hooer's da'ter, Mournin'.

Mrs. S. Why, la! messy on me, so he did!

Mrs. B. Why, did he marry a Hooer?

Mrs. S. Why, to be sure he did.—You knew Mournin'.

Mrs. B. Oh, mighty well; but I'd forgot that brother Smith married her: I really thought he married a Ramsbottom.

Mrs. R. Oh no, bless your soul, honey, he married Mournin'.

Mrs. B. Well, the law me, I'm clear beat!

Mrs. S. Oh it's so, you may be sure it is.

Mrs. B. Emp, emph, emph, emph! And brother Smith married Mournin' Hooer! Well, I'm clear put out! Seems to me I'm gittin' mighty forgetful some how.

Mrs. S. Oh yes, he married Mournin', and I saw her when she joined society.

Mrs. B. Why, you don't tell me so!

Mrs. S. Oh it's the truth. She did'nt join till after she was married, and the church took on mightily about his marrying one out of society. But after she joined they all got satisfied.

Mrs. R. Why, la! me, the seven stars is 'way over here!

Mrs. B. Well, let's light our pipes, and take a short smoke, and go to bed. How did you come on raisin' chickens this year, Mis' Shad?

Mrs. S. La messy, honey! I have had mighty bad luck. I had the prettiest pa'sel you most ever seed till the varment took to killin' 'em.

Mrs. R. and Mrs. B. The varment!!

Mrs. S. Oh dear, yes. The hawk catched a powerful sight of them; and then the varment took to 'em, and nat'ly took 'em fore and aft, bodily, till they left most none at all hardly. Sucky counted 'em up t'other day, and there war'nt but thirty-nine, she said, countin' in the old speckle hen's chickens that jist come off of her nest.

Mrs. R. and Mrs. B. Humph-h-h-h-!

Mrs. R. Well, I've had bad luck too. Billy's hound-dogs broke up most all my nests.

Mrs. B. Well, so they did me, Mis' Reed. I always did despise a hound-dog upon the face of yea'th.

Mrs. R. Oh, they're the bawllinest, squallinest, thievishest things ever was about one; but Billy will have 'em, and I think in my soul his old Troup's the beat of all creaters I ever seed in all my born days a suckin' o' hen's eggs—He's clean most broke me up entirely.

Mrs. S. The lackaday!

Mrs. R. And them that was hatched out, some took to

takin' the gaps, and some the pip, and one ailment or other, till they most all died.

Mrs. S. Well I reckon there must be somethin' in the season this year, that an't good for fowls; for Larkin Goodman's brother Jimme's wife's aunt Penny, told me, she lost most all her fowls with different sorts of ailments, the like of which she never seed before—They'd jist go 'long lookin, right well, and tilt right over backwards, (*Mrs. B.* The law!) and die right away, (*Mrs. R.* Did ever!) with a sort o' somethin' like the blind staggers.

Mrs. B. and Mrs. R. Messy on me!

Mrs. B. I reckon they must have eat somethin' did'nt agree with them.

Mrs. S. No they did'nt, for she fed 'em every mornin' with her own hand.

Mrs. B. Well, it's mighty curious!

A short pause ensued, which was broken by Mrs. Barney, with—"And brother Smith married Mournin' Hooer!" It came like an opiate upon my senses, and I dropt asleep.

The next morning, when we rose from our beds, we found the good ladies sitting round the fire just as I left them, for they rose long before us.

Mrs. Barney was just in the act of ejaculating, "And brother Smith married Mournin' "—when she was interrupted by our entry into the dining room. We were hardly seated, before Mrs. Reed began to verify her promise. "Mr. ————," said she to Ned, "did'nt you say last night, that them was two *men* that got married to one another?"

"Yes madam," said Ned.

"And did'nt you say they raised a fine pa'cel of children?"

"Yes madam, except Billy.—I said, you know, that he was a little wild."

"Well, yes; I know you said Billy was'nt as clever as the rest of them. But we old women were talking about it last night after you went out, and none of us could make it out, how they could have children; and I said, I reckoned you would'nt mind an old woman's chat; and, therefore, that I would ask you how it could be? I suppose you won't mind telling an old woman how it was."

"Certainly not, madam. They were both widowers before they fell in love with each other and got married."

"The lack-a-day! I wonder none of us thought o' that. And they had children before they got married?"

"Yes madam; they had none afterwards that I heard of."

We were here informed that our horses were in waiting, and we bade the good ladies farewell.

BALDWIN.

THE SHOOTING MATCH.

SHOOTING matches are probably nearly coeval with the colonization of Georgia. They are still common throughout the Southern States; though they are not as common as they were twenty-five or thirty years ago. Chance led me to one about a year ago. I was traveling in one of the north-eastern counties, when I overtook a swarthy, bright-

eyed, smerky little fellow, riding a small pony, and bearing
on his shoulder a long heavy rifle, which, judging from its
looks, I should say had done service in Morgan's corps.

"Good morning, sir!" said I, reining up my horse as I
came beside him.

"How goes it stranger?" said he, with a tone of independence and self-confidence, that awaked my curiosity to
know a little of his character.

"Going driving?" inquired I.

"Not exactly," replied he, surveying my horse with a
quizzical smile, "I have n't been a driving *by myself* for a year
or two, and my nose has got so bad lately I can't carry a
cold trail *without hounds to help me.*"

Alone, and without hounds, as he was, the question was
rather a silly one; but it answered the purpose for which it
was put, which was only to draw him into conversation, and
I proceeded to make as decent a retreat as I could.

"I did n't know," said I, "but that you were going to
meet the huntsmen, or going to your stand."

"Ah, sure enough," rejoined he, "that *mout* be a bee, as
the old woman said when she killed a wasp. It seems to me I
ought to know you."

"Well, if you *ought*, why *don't* you?"

"What *mout* your name be?"

"It *might* be any thing," said I, with borrowed wit; for I
knew my man, and knew what kind of conversation would
please him most.

"Well, what *is* it then?"

"It *is*, Hall," said I; "but you know it might as well have
been any thing else."

"Pretty digging!" said he. "I find you're not the fool I

took you to be; so here's to a better acquaintance with you."

"With all my heart," returned I; "but you must be as clever as I've been, and give me your name."

"To be sure I will, my old coon—take it—take it, and welcome. Any thing else about me you'd like to have?"

"No," said I, "there's nothing else about you worth having."

"Oh, yes there is, stranger! Do you see this?" holding up his ponderous rifle with an ease that astonished me. "If you will go with me to the shooting match, and see me knock out the *bull's-eye* with her a few times, you'll agree the old *Soap-stick's* worth something when Billy Curlew puts his shoulder to her."

This short sentence was replete with information to me. It taught me that my companion was *Billy Curlew;* that he was going to a *Shooting match;* that he called his rifle the *Soap-stick,* and that he was very confident of winning beef with her; or, which is nearly, but not quite the same thing, *driving the cross with her.*

"Well," said I, "if the shooting match is not too far out of my way, I'll go to it with pleasure."

"Unless your way lies through the woods from here," said Billy, "it'll not be much out of your way; for it's only a mile ahead of us, and there is no other road for you to take, till you get there; and as that thing you're riding in, an't well suited to fast travelling, among brushy knobs, I reckon you won't lose much by going by. I reckon you hardly ever was at a shooting match, stranger, from the cut of your coat?"

"Oh yes," returned I, "many a time. I won beef at one,

when I was hardly old enough to hold a shot-gun off-hand.''

"*Children* don't go to shooting matches about here," said he, with a smile of incredulity. "I never heard of but one that did, and he was a little *swinge*-cat.—He was born a shooting, and killed squirrels before he was weaned.''

"Nor did *I* ever hear of but one," replied I, "and that one was myself.''

"And where did you win beef so young, stranger?''

"At Berry Adams'.''

"Why stop, stranger, let me look at you good! Is your name *Lyman* Hall?''

"The very same," said I.

"Well, dang my buttons, if you an't the very boy my daddy used to tell me about. I was too young to recollect you myself; but I've heard daddy talk about you many a time. I believe mammy's got a neck-handkerchief now, that daddy won on your shooting at Collen Reid's store, when you were hardly knee high. Come along Lyman, and I'll go my death upon you at the shooting match, with the old Soap-stick at your shoulder.''

"Ah, Billy," said I, "the old Soap-stick will do much better at your own shoulder. It was my mother's notion, that sent me to the shooting match at Berry Adams'; and to tell you the honest truth, it was altogether a chance shot that made me win beef; but that was n't generally known; and most every body believed that I was carried there on account of my skill in shooting; and my fame was spread far and wide, I well remember. I remember too, perfectly well, your father's bet on me, at the store. *He* was at the shooting match, and nothing could make him believe, but that I was a great shot with a rifle, as well as a shot-gun. Bet he would, on me, in spite of all I could say; though I assured him, that I had never shot a rifle in my life. It so happened too, that there were but two bullets, or rather, a bullet and a half; and so confident was your father in my skill, that he made me shoot the half bullet; and, strange to tell, by another chance shot I like to have drove the cross, and won his bet."

"Now I know you're the very chap; for I heard daddy tell that very thing about the half bullet. Don't say any thing about it, Lyman, and durn my old shoes if I don't tear the lint off the boys with you at the shooting match. They'll never 'spect such a looking man as you are of knowing any thing about a rifle. I'll risk your *chance* shots."

I soon discovered that the father had eaten sour grapes, and the son's teeth were on edge; for Billy was just as incorrigibly obstinate, in his belief of my dexterity with a rifle, as his father had been before him.

We soon reached the place appointed for the shooting match. It went by the name of Sims' Cross Roads; because, here two roads intersected each other; and because, from the time that the first had been laid out, Archibald Sims had resided there. Archibald had been a Justice of the Peace in his day; (and where is the man of his age in Georgia who has not?) consequently he was called *'Squire* Sims. It is the custom in this State, when a man has once acquired a title, civil or military, to force it upon him as long as he lives; hence the countless number of titled personages, who are introduced in these sketches.

We stopt at the 'Squire's door. Billy hastily dismounted, gave me the shake of the hand which he had been reluctantly reserving for a mile back; and, leading me up to the 'Squire, thus introduced me: "Uncle Archy, this is Lyman

Hall; and for all you see him in these fine clothes, he's a *swinge*-cat—a darn sight cleverer fellow than he looks to be. Wait till you see him lift the old Soap-stick, and draw a bead upon the bull's-eye. You *gwine* to see fun here to-day— Don't say nothing about it."

"Well, Mr. Swinge-cat," said the 'Squire, "here's to a better acquaintance with you," offering me his hand.

"How goes it, uncle Archy?" said I, taking his hand warmly; (for I am always free and easy with those who are so with me; and in this course I rarely fail to please)— "How's the old woman?"

"Egad," said the 'Squire, chuckling, "there you're too hard for me; for she died two and twenty years ago, and I have n't heard a word from her since."

"What! and you never married again!"

"Never, as God's my Judge!" (a solemn asseveration truly, upon so light a subject.)

"Well, that's not my fault."

"No, nor it's not mine *ni*ther," said the 'Squire.

Here we were interrupted by the cry of another Ransy Sniffle—"Hello here! All you as wish to put in for the shoot'n match, come on here! for the putt'n in's *riddy* to begin."

About sixty persons, including mere spectators, had collected; the most of whom were more or less obedient to the call of Mealy Whitecotton—for that was the name of the self-constituted commander-in-chief. Some hastened, and some loitered, as they desired to be first or last on the list; for they shoot in the order in which their names are entered.

The beef was not present, nor is it ever upon such occasions; but several of the company had seen it, who all concurred in the opinion that it was a good beef, and well worth the price that was set upon it—eleven dollars. A general enquiry ran round, in order to form some opinion as to the number of shots that would be taken; for, of course, the price of a shot is cheapened in proportion to the increase of that number. It was soon ascertained that not more than twenty persons would take chances; but these twenty agreed to take the number of shots, at twenty-five cents each.

The competitors now began to give in their names; some for one, some for two, three, and a few for as many as four shots.

Billy Curlew hung back to the last; and when the list was offered to him, five shots remained undisposed of.

"How many shots left?" inquired Billy.

"Five," was the reply.

"Well, I take 'em all. Put down four shots to me, and one to Lyman Hall, paid for by William Curlew."

I was thunder struck—not at his proposition to pay for my shot, because I knew that Billy meant it as a token of friendship, and he would have been hurt if I had refused to let him do me this favor; but at the unexpected announcement of my name as a competitor for beef, at least one hundred miles from the place of my residence. I was prepared for a challenge from Billy to some of his neighbors for a *private* match upon me; but not for this.

I therefore protested against his putting in for me, and urged every reason to dissuade him from it, that I could, without wounding his feelings.

"Put it down!" said Billy, with the authority of an Emperor, and with a look that spoke volumes intelligible to every by-stander—"Reckon I don't know what I'm about?"

Then wheeling off, and muttering in an under, self-confi-
dent tone—"Dang old Roper," continued he, "if he don't
knock that cross to the north corner of creation and back
again before a cat can lick her foot."

Had I been the king of the cat tribe, they could not have
regarded me with more curious attention than did the
whole company from this moment. Every inch of me was
examined with the nicest scrutiny; and some plainly expressed by their looks, that they never would have taken me
for such a bite. I saw no alternative but to throw myself
upon a third chance shot; for though by the rules of the
sport I would have been allowed to shoot by proxy, by all
the rules of good breeding I was bound to shoot in person.
It would have been unpardonable, to disappoint the expectations, which had been raised on me. Unfortunately
too, for me, the match differed in one respect from those
which I had been in the habit of attending in my younger
days. In olden time the contest was carried on chiefly with
shot-guns, a generic term which, in those days, embraced
three descriptions of fire-arms—*Indian-traders*, (a long, cheap,
but sometimes excellent kind of gun, that mother Britain
used to send hither for traffic with the Indians,) *the large
Musket*, and the *Shot-gun*, properly so called. Rifles were,
however, always permitted to compete with them, under
equitable restrictions. These were, that they should be fired
off-hand, while the shot-guns were allowed a rest, the distance being equal; or that the distance should be one hundred yards for the rifle, to sixty, for the shot-gun, the mode
of firing being equal.

But this was a match of rifles exclusively; and these are
by far the most common at this time.

Most of the competitors fire at the same target; which is usually a board from nine inches to a foot wide, charred on one side as black as it can be made by fire without impairing materially the uniformity of its surface; on the darkened side of which is *pegged*, a square piece of white paper, which is larger or smaller, according to the distance at which it is to be placed from the marksmen. This is almost invariably sixty yards, and for it, the paper is reduced to about two and a half inches square. Out of the centre of it is cut a rhombus of about the width of an inch, measured diagonally—this is the *bull's-eye*, or *diamond*, as the marksmen choose to call it: in the centre of this is the cross. But every man is permitted to fix his target to his own taste; and accordingly, some remove one fourth of the paper, cutting from the centre of the square to the two lower corners; so as to leave a large angle opening from the centre downwards; while others reduce the angle more or less: but it is rarely the case that all are not satisfied with one of these figures.

The beef is divided into five prizes, or, as they are commonly termed, five *quarters*—the hide and tallow counting as one. For several years after the revolutionary war, a sixth was added; the *lead* which was shot in the match. This was the prize of the sixth best shot; and it used to be carefully extracted from the board, or tree, in which it was lodged, and afterwards remoulded. But this grew out of the exigency of the times, and has, I believe, been long since abandoned every where.

The three master shots, and rivals, were Moses Firmby, Larkin Spivey and Billy Curlew—to whom was added, upon this occasion, by common consent, and with awful forebodings—your humble servant.

The target was fixed, at an elevation of about three feet from the ground; and the judges (Captain Turner and Squire Porter) took their stands by it, joined by about half the spectators.

The first name on the catalogue was Mealy Whitecotton. Mealy stept out, rifle in hand, and toed the mark. His rifle was about three inches longer than himself, and near enough his own thickness to make the remark of Darby Chislom, as he stept out, tolerably appropriate—"Here comes the corn-stock and the sucker!" said Darby.

"Kiss my foot!" said Mealy. "The way I'll creep into that bull-eye's a fact."

"You'd better creep into your hind-sight," said Darby.

Mealy raised, and fired.

"A pretty good shot! Meal" said one. "Yes, a blamed good shot!" said a second. "Well done Meal!" said a third.

I was rejoiced when one of the company enquired, "Where is it?" for I could hardly believe they were founding these remarks upon the evidence of their senses. "Just on the right hand side of the bull's-eye," was the reply.

I looked with all the power of my eyes; but was unable to discover the least change in the surface of the paper. Their report, however, was true—so much keener is the vision of a practiced than unpracticed eye.

The next in order was Hiram Baugh. Hiram was like some race-horses which I have seen—he was too good, not to contend for every prize, and too good for nothing ever to win one.

"Gentlemen," said he, as he came to the mark, "I don't say that I'll win beef; but if my piece don't blow, I'll eat the paper; or be mighty apt to do it, if you'll b'lieve my racket.

My powder are not good powder, gentlemen—I bought it *thum* (from) Zeb. Daggett, and gin him three quarters of a dollar a pound for it; but it are not what I call good powder, gentlemen; but if old Buck-killer burns it clear, the boy you call Hiram Baugh eats paper, or comes mighty near it.''

"Well, blaze away," said Mealy, "and be ——— to you, and Zeb. Daggett and your powder and Buck-killer, and your powder-horn and shot-pouch to boot! How long you gwine stand thar talking 'fore you shoot?''

"Never mind," said Hiram, "I can talk a little and shoot a little too; but that's nothin'—Here goes!''

Hiram assumed the figure of a note of interrogation—took a long sight, and fired.

"I've eat paper," said he, at the crack of the gun, without looking, or seeming to look towards the target. "Buck-killer made a clear racket. Where am I, gentlemen?''

"You're just between Mealy and the diamond," was the reply.

"I said I'd eat paper, and I've done it; have'nt I, gentlemen?''

"And 'spose you have!" said Mealy, "what do that 'mount to? You'll not win beef, and never did.''

"Be that as it mout be, I've beat Meal. 'Cotton mighty easy; and the boy you call Hiram Baugh are able to do it.''

"And what do that 'mount to? Who the devil an't able to beat Meal. 'Cotton! I don't makes no pretense of bein' nothin' great, no how: but you always makes out as if you were gwine to keep 'em makin' crosses for you constant; and then do nothin' but '*eat paper*' at last; and that's a long way from *eatin' beef*, 'cordin' to Meal. 'Cotton's notions, as you call him.''

Simon Stow was now called on.

"Oh Lord!" exclaimed two or three: "Now we have it. It'll take him as long to shoot as it would take Squire Dobbins to run round a *track* o' land."

"Good-by, boys," said Bob Martin.

"Where you going Bob?"

"Going to gather in my crop—I'll be back agin though by the time Sime. Stow shoots."

Simon was used to all this, and therefore it did not disconcert him in the least. He went off and brought his own target, and set it up with his own hand.

He then wiped out his rifle—rubbed the pan with his hat —drew a piece of tow through the touch-hole with his wiper —filled his charger with great care—poured the powder into the rifle with equal caution—shoved in with his finger the two or three vagrant grains that lodged round the mouth of his piece—took out a handful of bullets—looked them all over carefully—selected one without flaw or wrinkle—drew out his patching—found the most even part of it —sprung open the grease-box in the breech of his rifle— took up just so much grease—distributed it with great equality over the chosen part of his patching—laid it over the muzzle of his rifle, grease side down—placed his ball upon it—pressed it a little—then took it up and turned the neck a little more perpendicularly downward—placed his knife-handle on it—just buried it in the mouth of the rifle— cut off the redundant patching just above the bullet— looked at it, and shook his head, in token that he had cut off too much or too little, no one knew which—sent down the ball—measured the contents of his gun with his first and second fingers, on the protruding part of the ramrod—

shook his head again, to signify there was too much or too little powder—primed carefully— placed an arched piece of tin over the hind sight to shade it—took his place—got a friend to hold his hat over the fore-sight to shade it—took a very long sight—fired—and did'nt even eat the paper.

"My piece was badly *loadned*," said Simon, when he learned the place of his ball.

"Oh, you did'nt take time," said Mealy. "No man can shoot that's in such a hurry as you is. I'd hardly got to sleep 'fore I heard the crack o' the gun."

The next was Moses Firmby. He was a tall, slim man, of rather sallow complexion; and it is a singular fact, that though probably no part of the world is more healthy than the mountainous region of Georgia, the mountaineers have not generally robust frames or fine complexions: they are, however, almost inexhaustible by toil.

Moses kept us not long in suspense. His rifle was already charged, and he fixed it upon the target, with a steadiness of nerve and aim that was astonishing to me and alarming to all the rest. A few seconds, and the report of his rifle broke the deathlike silence which prevailed.

"No great harm done yet," said Spivey, manifestly relieved from anxiety by an event which seemed to me better calculated to produce despair. Firmby's ball had cut out the lower angle of the diamond, directly on a right line with the cross.

Three or four followed him without bettering his shot; all of whom, however, with one exception, "eat the paper."

It now came to Spivey's turn. There was nothing remarkable in his person or manner. He took his place, lowered his rifle slowly from a perpendicular, until it came on a line with the mark—held it there like a vise for a moment, and fired.

"Pretty *sevigrous*, but nothing killing yet," said Billy Curlew, as he learned the place of Spivey's ball.

Spivey's ball had just broken the upper angle of the diamond; beating Firmby about half its width.

A few more shots, in which there was nothing remarkable, brought us to Billy Curlew. Billy stept out with much confidence; and brought the Soap-stick to an order, while he deliberately rolled up his shirt sleeves. Had I judged of Billy's chance of success from the looks of his gun, I should have said it was hopeless. The stock of Soap-stick seemed to have been made with a case knife; and had it been, the tool would have been but a poor apology for its clumsy appearance. An augur hole in the breech, served for a grease-box —a cotton string assisted a single screw in holding on the lock; and the thimbles were made, one of brass, one of iron, and one of tin.

"Where's Lark. Spivey's bullet?" called out Billy to the judges, as he finished rolling up his sleeves.

"About three quarters of an inch from the cross," was the reply.

"Well, clear the way! the Soap-stick's coming, and she'll be along in there among 'em presently."

Billy now planted himself astraddle, like an inverted V— shot forward his left hip—drew his body back to an angle of about forty-five degrees with the plane of the horizon— brought his cheek down close to the breech of old Soap-stick, and fixed her upon the mark with untrembling hand. His sight was long, and the swelling muscles of his left arm led me to believe that he was lessening his chance of success, with every half second that he kept it burdened with his ponderous rifle; but it neither flagged nor wavered until Soap-stick made her report.

"Where am I?" said Billy, as the smoke rose from before his eye.

"You've jist touched the cross on the lower side," was the reply of one of the judges.

"I was afraid I was drawing my bead a *leetle* too fine," said Billy. "Now, Lyman, you see what the Soap-stick can do.—Take her, and show the boys how you used to do when you was a baby."

I begged to reserve my shot to the last; pleading, rather sophistically, that it was in point of fact, one of Billy's shots. My plea was rather indulged than sustained, and the marksmen who had taken more than one shot, commenced the second round. This round was a manifest improvement upon the first. The cross was driven three times: once by Spivey, once by Firmby, and once by no less a personage than Mealy Whitecotton, whom chance seemed to favor for this time, merely that he might retaliate upon Hiram Baugh; and the bull's-eye was disfigued out of all shape.

The third and fourth rounds were shot. Billy discharged his last shot, which left the rights of parties thus: Billy Curlew first and fourth choice, Spivey second, Firmby third, and Whitecotton fifth. Some of my readers may perhaps be curious to learn, how a distinction comes to be made between several, all of whom drive the cross. The distinction is perfectly natural and equitable. Threads are stretched from the uneffaced parts of the once intersecting lines, by means of which the original position of the cross is precisely ascertained. Each bullet-hole being nicely pegged up as it is

made, it is easy to ascertain its circumference. To this, I believe they usually, if not invariably, measure, where none of
the balls touch the cross; but if the cross be driven, they
measure from it to the centre of the bullet-hole. To make a
draw shot, therefore, between two, who drive the cross, it is
necessary that the centre of both balls should pass directly
through the cross—a thing that very rarely happens.

The Bite alone remained to shoot. Billy wiped out his
rifle carefully, loaded her to the top of his skill, and handed
her to me. "Now," said he, "Lyman draw a fine bead, but
not too fine; for Soap-stick bears up her ball well. Take care
and don't touch the trigger, until you've got your bead; for
she's spring-trigger'd and goes mighty easy: but you hold
her to the place you want her, and if she don't go there dang
old Roper."

I took hold of Soap-stick, and lapsed immediately into
the most hopeless despair. I am sure I never handled as
heavy a gun in all my life. "Why Billy," said I, "you little
mortal you! what do you use such a gun as this for?"

"Look at the bull's-eye yonder!" said he.

"True," said I, "but *I* can't shoot her—it is impossible."

"Go long, you old coon!" said Billy, "I see what you're
at"—intimating that all this was merely to make the coming shot the more remarkable—"Daddy's little boy don't
shoot any thing but the old Soap-stick here to-day, I know."

The judges, I knew, were becoming impatient, and withal, my situation was growing more embarrassing every second; so I e'en resolved to try the Soap-stick without further
parley.

I stept out, and the most intense interest was excited all
around me, and it flashed like electricity around the target,

as I judged from the anxious gaze of all in that direction.

Policy dictated that I should fire with a falling rifle, and I adopted this mode; determining to fire as soon as the sights came on a line with the diamond, *bead* or no *bead*. Accordingly I commenced lowering old Soap-stick; but, in spite of all my muscular powers, she was strictly obedient to the laws of gravitation, and came down with a uniformly accelerated velocity. Before I could arrest her downward flight, she had not only passed the target, but was making rapid encroachments on my own toes.

"Why, he's the weakest man in the arms I ever seed," said one in a half whisper.

"It's only his fun," said Billy: "I know him."

"It may be fun," said the other; "but it looks mightily like yearnest to a man up a tree."

I now, of course, determined to reverse the mode of firing, and put forth all my physical energies to raise Soap-stick to the mark. The effort silenced Billy, and gave tongue to all his companions. I had just strength enough to master Soap-stick's obstinate proclivity, and consequently my nerves began to exhibit palpable signs of distress with her first imperceptible movement upward. A trembling commenced in my arms—increased, and extended rapidly to my body and lower extremities; so that by the time that I brought Soap-stick up to the mark, I was shaking from head to foot, exactly like a man under the continued action of a strong galvanic battery. In the mean time my friends gave vent to their feelings freely.

"I swear poin' blank," said one, "that man can't shoot."

"He used to shoot well," said another; "but can't now nor never could."

"You better *git* away from 'bout that mark!" bawled a third, "for I'll be dod durned if Broadcloth don't give some of you the dry gripes if you stand too close thare."

"The stranger's got the *peedoddles*,"* said a fourth, with humorous gravity.

"If he had bullets enough in his gun, he'd shoot a ring round the bull's-eye big as a spinning-wheel," said a fifth.

As soon as I found that Soap-stick was high enough, (for I made no further use of the sights than to ascertain this fact,) I pulled trigger, and off she went. I have always found that the most creditable way of relieving myself of derision, was to heighten it myself as much as possible. It is a good plan in all circles, but by far the best which can be adopted among the plain rough farmers of the country. Accordingly I brought old Soap-stick to an order, with an air of triumph —tipt Billy a wink, and observed, "Now Billy 's your time to make your fortune—Bet 'em two to one that I've knocked out the cross."

"No, I'll be dod blamed if I do," said Billy; "but I'll bet you two to one you han't hit the plank."

"Ah, Billy," said I, "I was joking about *betting*, for I never bet; nor would I have you to bet: indeed I do not feel exactly right in shooting for beef; for it is a species of gaming at last: but I'll say this much—if that cross is'nt knocked out, I'll never shoot for beef again as long as I live."

"By dod," said Mealy Whitecotton, "you'll lose no great things at that."

"Well," said I, "I reckon I know a little about wabbling.

* This word was entirely new to me; but like most, if not all words, in use among the common people, it is doubtless a legitimate English word, or rather a compound of two words, the last a little corrupted, and was very aptly applied in this instance. It is a compound of "*pee*," to peep with one eye, and "*daddle*," to totter, or wabble.

Is it possible, Billy, a man who shoots as well as you do, never practiced shooting with the double wabble? It's the greatest take in, in the world, when you learn to drive the cross with it. Another sort for getting bets upon, to the drop-sight, with a single wabble! And the Soap-stick's the very yarn for it."

"Tell you what, stranger," said one, "you're too hard for us all here. We never *hearn* o' that sort o' shoot'n in these parts."

"Well," returned I, "you've seen it now, and I'm the boy that can do it."

The judges were now approaching with the target, and a singular combination of circumstances had kept all my party in utter ignorance of the result of my shot. Those about the target had been prepared by Billy Curlew for a great shot from me; their expectations had received assurance from the courtesy which had been extended to me; and nothing had happened to disappoint them, but the single caution to them against the "dry gripes," which was as likely to have been given in irony as in earnest; for my agonies under the weight of the Soap-stick, were either imperceptible to them at the distance of sixty yards, or, being visible, were taken as the flourishes of an expert who wished to "astonish the natives." The other party did not think the direction of my ball worth the trouble of a question; or, if they did, my airs and harangue had put the thought to flight before it was delivered. Consequently they were all transfixed with astonishment when the judges presented the target to them, and gravely observed—"It's only second best after all the fuss." "Second best!" exclaimed I, with uncontrollable transports. The whole of my party rushed to the target to have the evidence of their senses before they would believe the report: but most marvellous fortune decreed that it should be true. Their incredulity and astonishment were most fortunate for me; for they blinded my hearers to the real feelings with which the exclamation was uttered, and allowed me sufficient time to prepare myself for making the best use of what I had said before, with a very different object.

"Second best!" reiterated I, with an air of despondency, as the company turned from the target to me.—"Second best only! Here Billy, my son, take the old Soap-stick; she's a good piece, but I'm getting too old and dim sighted to shoot a rifle; especially with the drop-sight and double wabbles."

"Why good Lord a'mighty!" said Billy, with a look that baffles all description, "an't you *driv* the cross!"

"Oh, driv the cross!" rejoined I, carelessly. "What's that! Just look where my ball is! I do believe in my soul its centre is a full quarter of an inch from the cross. I wanted to lay the centre of the bullet upon the cross, just as if you'd put it there with your fingers."

Several received this palaver with a contemptuous but very appropriate curl of the nose; and Mealy Whitecotton offered to bet a half pint, "that I could'nt do the like agin with no sort o' wabbles, he did'nt care what." But I had already fortified myself on this quarter, by my morality. A decided majority, however, were clearly of opinion that I was serious; and they regarded me as one of the wonders of the world. Billy increased the majority by now coming out fully with my history, as he had received it from his father; to which I listened with quite as much astonishment as any

other one of his hearers. He begged me to go home with him
for the night, or as he expressed it, "to go home with him
and swap lies that night, and it should'nt cost me a cent,"
the true reading of which, is, that if I would go home with
him, and give him the pleasure of an evening's chat about
old times, his house should be as free to me as my own. But
I could not accept his hospitality without retracing five or
six miles of the road which I had already passed; and therefore I declined it.

"Well, if you won't go, what must I tell the old woman
for you? for she'll be mighty glad to hear from the boy that
won the silk handkerchief for her, and I expect she'll lick
me for not bringing you home with me."

"Tell her," said I, "that I send her a quarter of beef,
which I won, as I did the handkerchief, by nothing in the
world but mere good luck."

"Hold your jaw, Lyman!" said Billy, "I an't a gwine to
tell the old woman any such lies; for she's a *real* reg'lar
built Meth'dist."

As I turned to depart, "Stop a minute, stranger!" said
one: then lowering his voice to a confidential but distinctly
audible tone, "what you offering for?" continued he. I assured him I was not a candidate for any thing—that I had
accidentally fallen in with Billy Curlew, who begged me to
come with him to the shooting match, and as it lay right on
my road, I had stopped. "Oh," said he, with a conciliatory
nod, "if you're up for any thing you need'nt be mealy-
mouthed about it, 'fore us boys; for we'll all go in for you
here up to the handle." "Yes," said Billy, "dang old Roper if
we don't go our death for you, no matter who offers. If ever
you come out for any thing, Lyman, jist let the boys of Up-

per Hogthief know it, and they'll go for you, to the hilt, against creation, tit or no tit, that's the *tatur*." I thanked them kindly, but repeated my assurances. The reader will not suppose that the district took its name from the character of the inhabitants. In almost every county in the State, there is some spot, or district, which bears a contemptuous appellation, usually derived from local rivalships, or from a single accidental circumstance.

HALL.

FINIS.

Georgia Scenes was first published in 1835 at the *State Rights Sentinel* printing office, Augusta. The illustrations are from the second edition, published by Harper and Brothers in 1840. Richard Harwell is Librarian at Georgia Southern College, Statesboro. § This book was planned and edited at Savannah, Georgia, by The Beehive Press, which publishes books about Georgia and the South. Its pressmark, which appears above and pictures bees busy at their hive, expresses the enthusiasm of this work; the source of the pressmark—an early Georgia colonial pamphlet entitled *An Impartial Enquiry into the State and Utility of the Province of Georgia*, London, 1741—suggests a spirit of free intellectual endeavor. § This book was printed by The Stinehour Press at Lunenburg, Vermont, for

THE BEEHIVE PRESS
321 Barnard Street
Savannah, Georgia 31401